To:

_____

From:

_____

Date:

_____

Message:

_____

_____

_____

A BOOK OF Prayer

STORMIE OMARTIAN

HARVEST HOUSE PUBLISHERS

EUGENE, OREGON

Cover by Koechel Peterson & Associates, Inc., Minneapolis, Minnesota

Backcover author photo © Harry Langdon

A BOOK OF PRAYER
Copyright © 2006 by Stormie Omartian
Published by Harvest House Publishers
Eugene, Oregon 97402
www.harvesthousepublishers.com

ISBN 978-0-7369-1722-3

Library of Congress Cataloging-in-Publication Data
Omartian, Stormie.
  A book of prayer / Stormie Omartian.
      p. cm.
    ISBN-13: 978-0-7369-1722-3 (pbk.)
    ISBN-10: 0-7369-1722-5
  1. Prayers. I. Title.
    BV245.O54 2006
    242—dc22   2005019209

Contents

Introduction

Life is much better when prayer is an ongoing part of it. It helps if we can take a few moments at various times throughout each of our busy days to pause for a refreshing and comforting time of communicating with our heavenly Father. And also to set our heart right with a word from His Holy Scripture. It is my hope that this book of prayer will help you to do all that.

Many of the following 365 prayers are from my books on prayer, although I wrote some of the prayers included here especially for this book. They were chosen with the intention of helping you focus your prayers on different areas of your life that you might not think to pray about that day. And it is always my desire that these short prayers will motivate you to move into more extensive prayer and to spend more time with the Lord, who loves you so much that He wants to hear what is on your heart and move powerfully in your life.

Stormie Omartian

PART I

The Power
of a
PRAYING
WOMAN

Lord, Draw Me into a Closer Walk with You

*L*ord, I draw close to You today, grateful that You will draw close to me as You have promised in Your Word (James 4:8). I long to dwell in Your presence, and I want to know You in every way You can be known. Teach me what I need to learn in order to know You better. I don't want to be a person who is always learning and never able to come to the knowledge of the truth (2 Timothy 3:7). I want to know the truth about who You are, because I know that You are near to all who call upon You in truth (Psalm 145:18).

I will pray the Father, and He will give you another Helper, that He may abide with you forever—the Spirit of truth, whom the world cannot receive, because it neither sees Him nor knows Him; but you know Him, for He dwells with you and will be in you.

JOHN 14:16-17

Lord, Draw Me into a Closer Walk with You

Lord, thank You for the pastors and spiritual leaders who have input into my life. Help me to glean knowledge and understanding of Your ways from them so that I can know You better. Bless them and help them to always be the men and women of God You created them to be.

I will give you shepherds according to My heart, who will feed you with knowledge and understanding.

JEREMIAH 3:15

Lord, Draw Me into a Closer Walk with You

❧

*L*ord, help me to set aside time each day to meet with You alone. As I come before You, teach me to pray the way You want me to. Help me to learn more about You. Lord, You have said, If anyone thirsts, let him come to Me and drink (John 7:37). I thirst for more of You because I am in a dry place without You. I come to You this day and drink deeply of Your Spirit. I know You are everywhere, but I also know there are deeper manifestations of Your presence that I long to experience. Draw me close as I draw near to you, so that I may dwell in Your presence like never before.

❧

Draw near to God and He will draw near to you.

JAMES 4:8

Lord, Cleanse Me and Make My Heart Right Before You

*L*ord, I come humbly before You and ask You to cleanse my heart and renew a right spirit within me. Forgive me for thoughts I have had, words I have spoken, and things that I have done that are not glorifying to You or are in direct contradiction to Your commands. Specifically, I confess to You (name any thoughts, words, or actions that you know are not pleasing to God). I confess it as sin and I repent of it. I choose to walk away from this pattern of thought or action and live Your way. I know that You are gracious and merciful, slow to anger and of great kindness (Joel 2:13). Forgive me for ever taking that for granted.

If we confess our sins, He is faithful and just to forgive us our sins and to cleanse us from all unrighteousness.

1 JOHN 1:9

Lord, Cleanse Me and Make My Heart Right Before You

*L*ord, show me any sin in my life so that I can confess it to You and be cleansed. Keep me undeceived in my heart and mind. Where I have sinned against You, I ask You to forgive and restore me. Show me if I need to confess my mistakes to anyone else so that the air can be cleared between us.

Confess your trespasses to one another, and pray for one another, that you may be healed.

JAMES 5:16

Lord, Cleanse Me and Make My Heart Right Before You

Lord, I pray that you will have mercy upon me, O God, according to Your lovingkindness; according to the multitude of Your tender mercies, blot out my transgressions. Create in me a clean heart, and renew a steadfast spirit within me. Do not cast me away from Your presence, and do not take Your Holy Spirit from me (Psalm 51:1,10-11). See if there is any wicked way in me, and lead me in the way everlasting (Psalm 139:24). Show me the truth about myself so that I can see it clearly. Make me clean and right before You. I want Your forgiveness so that times of refreshing may come from Your presence (Acts 3:19).

I acknowledged my sin to You, and my iniquity I have not hidden. I said, I will confess my transgressions to the LORD, and You forgave the iniquity of my sin.

PSALM 32:5

Lord, Cleanse Me and Make My Heart Right Before You

*L*ord, "wash me thoroughly from my iniquity, and cleanse me from my sin" (Psalm 51:1-2). "Cleanse me from secret faults" (Psalm 19:12). I realize that You are a God who "knows the secrets of the heart" (Psalm 44:21). Show me any place in my life where I harbor sin in thoughts, words, or actions that I have not recognized. Examine my soul and expose my motives to reveal what I need to understand. Enable me to make changes where I need to do so. Open my eyes to what I need to see so that I can confess all sin and repent of it. I want to cleanse my hands and purify my heart as You have commanded in Your Word (James 4:8).

If our heart does not condemn us, we have confidence toward God. And whatever we ask we receive from Him, because we keep His commandments and do those things that are pleasing in His sight.

1 JOHN 3:21-22

Lord, Help Me to Be a Forgiving Person

*L*ord, help me to forgive others. If I have any anger, bitterness, resentment, or unforgiveness that I am not recognizing, reveal it to me and I will confess it to You as sin. Specifically, I ask You to help me fully forgive (name anyone you feel you need to forgive). Make me to understand the depth of Your forgiveness toward me so that I won't hold back forgiveness from others. I realize that my forgiving someone doesn't make them right; it makes me free. I also realize that You are the only one who knows the whole story, and You will see justice done.

The discretion of a man makes him slow to anger, and his glory is to overlook a transgression.

PROVERBS 19:11

Lord, Help Me to Be a Forgiving Person

ᘓᕼ᠐ᕼᘔ

*L*ord, I don't want anything to come between You and me, and I don't want my prayers to be hindered because I have entertained sin in my heart. I choose this day to forgive everyone and everything, and walk free from the death that unforgiveness brings. If any person has unforgiveness toward me, I pray You would soften their heart to forgive me and show me what I can do to help resolve this issue between us. I know that I cannot be a light to others as long as I am walking in the darkness of unforgiveness. I choose to walk in the light as You are in the light and be cleansed from all sin (1 John 1:7).

ᕼᘔᕽ

Judge not, and you shall not be judged. Condemn not, and you shall not be condemned. Forgive, and you will be forgiven.

LUKE 6:37

Lord, Help Me to Be a Forgiving Person

*L*ord, if I have blamed You for things that have happened in my life, show me so I can confess it before You. Enable me to love my enemies as You have commanded in Your Word. Teach me to bless those who curse me and persecute me (Matthew 5:44-45). Remind me to pray for those who hurt or offend me so that my heart will be soft toward them. I don't want to become hard and bitter because of unforgiveness. Make me a person who is quick to forgive. Where there is distance between me and any other family member because of unforgiveness, I pray You would break down that wall. Help me to forgive every time I need to do so.

Love your enemies, bless those who curse you, do good to those who hate you, and pray for those who spitefully use you and persecute you, that you may be sons of your Father in heaven.

MATTHEW 5:44-45

Lord, Teach Me to Walk in Obedience to Your Ways

Lord, Your Word says that those of us who love Your law will have great peace and nothing will cause us to stumble (Psalm 119:165). I love Your law because I know it is good and it is there for my benefit. Enable me to live in obedience to each part of it so that I will not stumble and fall. Help me to obey You so that I can dwell in the confidence and peace of knowing I am living Your way. My heart wants to obey You in all things, Lord. Please show me where I am not doing that. "With my whole heart I have sought You; oh, let me not wander from Your commandments!" (Psalm 119:10).

He who has My commandments and keeps them, it is he who loves Me. And he who loves Me will be loved by My Father, and I will love him and manifest Myself to him.

JOHN 14:21

Lord, Teach Me to Walk in Obedience to Your Ways

*L*ord, Your Word says that if we say we have no sin, we deceive ourselves, and the truth is not in us (1 John 1:8). I don't want to deceive myself by not asking You where I am missing the mark You have set for my life. Show me if I'm doing things I should not. Help me to hear Your specific instructions to me. Speak to me clearly through Your Word so I will know what's right and what's wrong. I don't want to grieve the Holy Spirit in anything I do (Ephesians 4:30). Help me to be ever learning about Your ways so I can live in the fullness of Your presence and move into all You have for me.

He who keeps His commandments abides in Him, and He in him. And by this we know that He abides in us, by the Spirit whom He has given us.

1 JOHN 3:24

Lord, Strengthen Me to Stand Against the Enemy

Lord, I thank You for suffering and dying on the cross for me, and for rising again to defeat death and hell. My enemy is defeated because of what You have done. Thank You that You have given me all authority over him (Luke 10:19). Show me when I am not recognizing the encroachment of the enemy in my life. Teach me to use that authority You have given me to see him defeated in every area. Help me to fast and pray regularly in order to break any stronghold the enemy is trying to erect in my life. By the power of Your Holy Spirit I can successfully resist the devil and he must flee from me (James 4:7).

Be strong in the Lord and in the power of His might. Put on the whole armor of God, that you may be able to stand against the wiles of the devil.

EPHESIANS 6:10-11

Lord, Strengthen Me
to Stand Against the Enemy

*L*ord, I pray You would bring righteous leaders into the forefront of decision making in our nation and give Your wisdom to each one of them. Destroy the strongholds and plans of the enemy *in* this country and *for* this country. Protect our military leaders and troops wherever they are. Give them revelation, guidance, and favor. Pour out your peace upon our nation.

I exhort first of all that supplications, prayers, intercessions, and giving of thanks be made for all men, for kings and all who are in authority, that we may lead a quiet and peaceable life in all godliness and reverence.

1 TIMOTHY 2:1-2

Lord, Strengthen Me to Stand Against the Enemy

∽∾∾∽

*L*ord, I know in the midst of the battle I don't have to be afraid in the face of the enemy (Deuteronomy 20:3). Thank you that even though the enemy tries to take me captive to do his will, You have given me the power to escape his snares completely (2 Timothy 2:26). Thank You that You are my shield because I live Your way (Proverbs 2:7). Help me to not be overcome by evil, but instead give me the strength to overcome evil with good (Romans 12:21). Hide me in the secret place of Your presence from the plots of evil men (Psalm 31:20). The enemy will never bring me down as long as I stand strong in You.

∾∾

When the whirlwind passes by, the wicked is no more, but the righteous has an everlasting foundation.

PROVERBS 10:25

Lord, Show Me How to Take Control of My Mind

Lord, I don't ever want to walk according to my own thinking (Isaiah 65:2). I want to bring every thought captive and control my mind. Your Word is a discerner of the thoughts and intents of the heart (Hebrews 4:12). As I read Your Word, may it reveal any wrong thinking in me. May Your Word be so etched in my mind that I will be able to identify a lie of the enemy the minute I hear it. Spirit of truth, keep me undeceived. I know You have given me authority over all the power of the enemy (Luke 10:19), and so I command the enemy to get away from my mind. I refuse to listen to his lies.

Be renewed in the spirit of your mind, and put on the new man which was created according to God, in true righteousness and holiness.

EPHESIANS 4:23-24

Lord, Show Me How to Take Control of My Mind

*L*ord, I don't want to think futile and foolish thoughts or give place to thoughts that are not glorifying to You (Romans 1:21). Thank You that I have the mind of Christ (1 Corinthians 2:16). I want Your thoughts to be my thoughts. Show me where I have filled my mind with anything that is ungodly. Help me to resist doing that and instead fill my mind with thoughts, words, music, and images that are glorifying to You. Help me to think upon what is true, noble, just, pure, lovely, of good report, virtuous, and praiseworthy (Philippians 4:8). I lay claim to the sound mind that You have given me (2 Timothy 1:7).

Do not be conformed to this world, but be transformed by the renewing of your mind, that you may prove what is that good and acceptable and perfect will of God.

ROMANS 12:2

Lord, Rule Me in Every Area of My Life

*L*ord, I bow before You this day and declare that You are Lord over every area of my life. I surrender myself and my life to You and invite You to rule in every part of my mind, soul, body and spirit. I love You with all my heart, with all my soul, and with all my mind. I commit to trusting You with my whole being. Enable me to deny myself in order to take up my cross daily and follow You (Luke 9:23). I want to be Your disciple just as You have said in Your Word (Luke 14:27). I want to lose my life in You so I can save it (Luke 9:24).

If we live, we live to the Lord; and if we die, we die to the Lord. Therefore, whether we live or die, we are the Lord's.

ROMANS 14:8

Lord, Rule Me
in Every Area of My Life

*H*eavenly Father, enable me and my friends and family to "be kindly affectionate to one another with brotherly love, in honor giving preference to one another; not lagging in diligence, fervent in spirit, serving the Lord; rejoicing in hope, patient in tribulation, continuing steadfastly in prayer" (Romans 12:10-12). Teach us how to love one another the way that You love us.

Let each of you look out not only for his own interests, but also for the interests of others.

PHILIPPIANS 2:4

Lord, Rule Me
in Every Area of My Life

*L*ord, my desire is to please You and hold nothing back. I surrender my relationships, my finances, my work, my recreation, my decisions, my time, my body, my mind, my soul, my desires, and my dreams. I put them all in Your hands to be used for Your glory. I declare this day that I have been crucified with Christ; it is no longer I who live, but Christ lives in me; and the life which I now live in the flesh I live by faith in the Son of God, who loved me and gave Himself for me (Galatians 2:20). Rule me in every area of my life, Lord, and lead me into all that You have for me.

As you have therefore received Christ Jesus the Lord, so walk in Him, rooted and built up in Him and established in the faith, as you have been taught, abounding in it with thanksgiving.

COLOSSIANS 2:6-7

Lord, Take Me
Deeper in Your Word

*L*ord, Your Word is a lamp to my feet and a light to my path (Psalm 119:105). Enable me to truly comprehend its deepest meaning. Give me greater understanding than I have ever had before, and reveal to me the hidden treasures buried there. I pray that I will have a heart that is teachable and open to what You want me to know. Change me as I read it. Help me to be diligent to put Your Word inside my soul faithfully every day. Show me where I'm wasting time that could be better spent reading Your Word. Give me the ability to memorize it. Etch it in my mind and heart so that it becomes a part of me.

He who looks into the perfect law of liberty and continues in it, and is not a forgetful hearer but a doer of the work, this one will be blessed in what he does.

JAMES 1:25

Lord, Take Me
Deeper in Your Word

*L*ord, teach me from Your Word so that I will know Your ways and walk in them. Help me to live in obedience to Your commands. Thank You that my sin doesn't have to separate me from You because by repenting of it and confessing it to You, I can be cleansed of my sins and set free.

If we confess our sins, He is faithful and just to forgive us our sins and to cleanse us from all unrighteousness.

1 JOHN 1:9

Lord, Take Me Deeper in Your Word

❧

*L*ord, may Your Word remind me of who You are and how much You love me. May it bring the security of knowing my life is in Your hands and You will supply all my needs. Thank You, Lord, that when I look into Your Word I find You. Give me ears to recognize Your voice speaking to me every time I read it (Mark 4:23). When I hear Your voice and follow You, my life is full. When I get off the path You have for me, my life is empty. Guide, perfect, and fill me with Your Word this day.

❧

Blessed is the man who walks not in the counsel of the ungodly, nor stands in the path of sinners, nor sits in the seat of the scornful; but his delight is in the law of the LORD, and in His law he meditates day and night. He shall be like a tree planted by the rivers of water that brings forth its fruit in its season, whose leaf also shall not wither; and whatever he does shall prosper.

PSALM 1:1-3

Lord, Take Me
Deeper in Your Word

*L*ord, I don't want to be just a hearer of Your Word. Show me how to be a doer of Your Word as well. Enable me to respond the way I should and obey You. Show me when I am not doing what it says. Help me to apply my heart to Your instruction and my ears to Your Words of knowledge (Proverbs 23:12). May Your Word correct my attitude and remind me of what my purpose is on earth. May it cleanse my heart and give me hope that I can rise above my limitations. It is food to my soul, and I can't live without it. Help me to know You better through Your Word.

Whoever keeps His word, truly the love of God is perfected in him. By this we know that we are in Him.

1 JOHN 2:5

Lord, Instruct Me as I
Put My Life in Right Order

⊷⊰⊷

*L*ord, I pray You would help me set my life in right order. I want to always put You first above all else in my life. Teach me how to love You with all my heart, mind, and soul. Show me when I am not doing that. Show me if I have lifted up my soul to an idol. My desire is to serve You and only You. Please help me to live accordingly.

⊷⊰⊷

Obey those who rule over you, and be submissive, for they watch out for your souls, as those who must give account. Let them do so with joy and not with grief, for that would be unprofitable for you.

HEBREWS 13:17

Lord, Instruct Me as I Put My Life in Right Order

*L*ord, help me to be in the church You want me to be in, so that I can become a part of the work You are doing there. I pray that I will always belong to a church that worships Your way. One that teaches Your Word in a clear and balanced manner and understands the power of prayer.

God has set the members, each one of them, in the body just as He pleased.

1 CORINTHIANS 12:18

Lord, Instruct Me as I Put My Life in Right Order

∞

*L*ord, help me to willingly submit myself to others where I need to do so. Show me clearly to whom I am to be submitted and how I am to do it. Give me discernment and wisdom about this. Show me any time I am not submitted to the right people in the right way. I know that if my life is not in proper order I will not receive the blessings You have for me. But I also know that if I seek You first, all that I need will be added to me (Matthew 6:33). I seek You first this day and ask that You would enable me to put my life in perfect order.

∞

He who finds his life will lose it, and he who loses his life for My sake will find it.

MATTHEW 10:39

Lord, Prepare Me to Be a True Worshiper

*L*ord, there is no source of greater joy for me than worshiping You. I come into Your presence with thanksgiving and bow before You this day. I exalt Your name, for You are great and worthy to be praised. You have put gladness in my heart (Psalm 4:7). All honor and majesty, strength and glory, holiness and righteousness are Yours, O Lord. You are gracious and full of compassion, slow to anger and great in mercy (Psalm 145:8). You are mighty in power and Your understanding is infinite (Psalm 147:5). You give food to the hungry and freedom to the prisoners. Thank You that You open the eyes of the blind and raise up those who are bowed down (Psalm 146:7-8).

Whoever offers praise glorifies Me; and to him who orders his conduct aright I will show the salvation of God.

PSALM 50:23

Lord, Prepare Me to Be a True Worshiper

ord, help me to be a praising person. I want to worship Your way. Instruct me in what I need to know about worship and prayer so that I can become the worshiper and intercessor You have called me to be. Help me to make worshiping You a way of life.

Oh come, let us worship and bow down; let us kneel before the LORD our Maker. For He is our God, and we are the people of His pasture, and the sheep of His hand.

PSALM 95:6-7

Lord, Prepare Me to Be a True Worshiper

*L*ord, teach me to worship You with my whole heart the way You want me to. Make me a true worshiper. May praise and worship of You be my first response to every circumstance. I praise Your name this day, Lord, for You are good and Your mercy endures forever (Psalm 136:1). Because Your lovingkindness is better than life, my lips shall praise You. Thus I will bless You while I live; I will lift up my hands in Your name (Psalm 63:3-4). I will declare Your glory among the nations and Your wonders among all peoples (Psalm 96:3). I worship You in the splendor of Your holiness and give You the glory due Your name (Psalm 29:2).

I will worship toward Your holy temple, and praise Your name for Your lovingkindness and Your truth; for You have magnified Your word above all Your name.

PSALM 138:2

Lord, Prepare Me to Be a True Worshiper

*L*ord, thank You that Your plans for my life are good, and You have a future for me that is full of hope. Thank You that You are always restoring my life to greater wholeness. I praise You and thank You that You are my Healer, my Deliverer, my Provider, my Redeemer, my Father, and my Comforter. Thank You for revealing Yourself to me through Your Word, through Your Son, Jesus, and through Your mighty works upon the earth and in my life. Thank You for Your love, peace, joy, faithfulness, grace, mercy, kindness, truth, and healing. Thank You that I can depend on You, for You and Your Word are unfailing. Thank You that You are the same yesterday, today, and tomorrow.

Let all those rejoice who put their trust in You; let them ever shout for joy, because You defend them; let those also who love Your name be joyful in You. For You, O LORD, will bless the righteous; with favor You will surround him as with a shield.

PSALM 5:11-12

Lord, Bless Me
in the Work I Do

*L*ord, I pray You would show me what work I am supposed to be doing. If it is something other than what I am doing now, reveal it to me. If it is something I am to do in addition to what I am already doing, show me that too. Whatever it is You have called me to do, both now and in the future, I pray You will give me the strength and energy to get it done well. May I find great fulfillment and satisfaction in every aspect of it, even the most difficult and unpleasant parts. Thank You that in all labor there is profit of one kind or another (Proverbs 14:23).

Blessed is every one who fears the Lord, who walks in His ways. When you eat the labor of your hands, you shall be happy, and it shall be well with you.

PSALM 128:1-2

Lord, Bless Me
in the Work I Do

*L*ord, I thank You for the abilities You have given me. Where I am lacking in skill help me to grow and improve so that I do my work well. Open doors of opportunity to use my skills and close doors that I am not to go through. Give me wisdom and direction about that. I commit my work to You, Lord, knowing You will establish it (Proverbs 16:3). May it always be that I love the work I do and be able to do the work I love. Establish the work of my hands so that what I do will find favor with others and be a blessing for many. May it always be glorifying to You.

Let the beauty of the LORD our God be upon us, and establish the work of our hands for us; yes, establish the work of our hands.

PSALM 90:17

Lord, Bless Me in the Work I Do

*L*ord, bless the people I work for and with. May I always be a blessing and a help to each one of them. As I come in contact with others in my work, I pray that Your love and peace will flow through me and speak loudly of Your goodness. Enable me to touch them for Your kingdom. Teach me to excel so that the result of what I do will be pleasing to others. Enable me to do what I do successfully. According to Your Word I pray that I will not lag in diligence in my work, but remain fervent in spirit, serving You in everything I do (Romans 12:11).

The blessing of the Lord makes one rich, and He adds no sorrow with it.

PROVERBS 10:22

Lord, Plant Me so I Will Bear the Fruit of Your Spirit

*L*ord, I pray You would plant the fruit of Your Spirit in me and cause it to flourish. Help me to abide in You, Jesus, so that I will bear fruit in my life. Holy Spirit, fill me afresh with Your love today so that it will flow out of me and into the lives of others. You said in Your Word to let the peace of Christ rule in your hearts (Colossians 3:15). I pray that Your peace would rule my heart and mind to such a degree that people would sense it when they are around me. Help me to pursue the things which make for peace and the things by which one may edify another (Romans 14:19).

The fruit of the Spirit is love, joy, peace, long-suffering, kindness, goodness, faithfulness, gentleness, self-control. Against such there is no law.

GALATIANS 5:22-23

Lord, Plant Me so I Will Bear the Fruit of Your Spirit

*L*ord, where I need to be pruned in order to bear more fruit, I submit myself to You. I know that without You I can do nothing. You are the vine and I am the branch. I must abide in You in order to bear fruit. Thank You for Your promise that if I abide in You and Your Word abides in me, I can ask what I desire and it will be done for me (John 15:7). Thank You for Your promise that says if I ask I will receive (John 16:24). May I be like a tree planted by the rivers of Your living water so that I will bring forth fruit in season that won't wither (Psalm 1:3).

By this My Father is glorified, that you bear much fruit; so you will be My disciples.

JOHN 15:8

Lord, Preserve Me
in Purity and Holiness

Lord, You have said in Your Word that You did not call me to uncleanness, but in holiness (1 Thessalonians 4:7). You chose me to be holy and blameless before You. I know that I have been washed clean and made holy by the blood of Jesus (1 Corinthians 6:11). You have clothed me in Your righteousness and enabled me to put on the new man in true righteousness and holiness (Ephesians 4:24). Help me to cling to what is good (Romans 12:9) and keep myself pure (1 Timothy 5:22). Lord, help me to separate myself from anything that is not holy. I don't want to waste my life on things that have no value.

He chose us in Him before the foundation of the world, that we should be holy and without blame before Him in love.

EPHESIANS 1:4

Lord, Preserve Me in Purity and Holiness

$\mathcal{L}$ord, help me to examine my ways so that I can return to Your ways wherever I have strayed. Enable me to take any steps necessary in order to be pure before You. I want to be holy as You are holy. Make me a partaker of Your holiness (Hebrews 12:10), and may my spirit, soul, and body be kept blameless (1 Thessalonians 5:23). I know that You have called me to purity and holiness, and You have said that He who calls you is faithful, who will also do it (1 Thessalonians 5:24). Thank You that You will keep me pure and holy so I will be fully prepared for all You have for me.

Blessed are the pure in heart, for they shall see God.

MATTHEW 5:8

Lord, Move Me into the Purpose for Which I Was Created

❧❧❧

*L*ord, I know Your plan for me existed before I knew You, and You will bring it to pass. Help me to walk worthy of the calling with which [I was] called (Ephesians 4:1). I know there is an appointed plan for me, and I have a destiny that will now be fulfilled. Help me to live my life with a sense of purpose and understanding of the calling You have given me. Take away any discouragement I may feel and replace it with joyful anticipation of what You are going to do through me. Use me as Your instrument to make a positive difference in the lives of those whom You put in my path.

❧❧❧

Be even more diligent to make your call and election sure, for if you do these things you will never stumble.

2 PETER 1:10

Lord, Move Me into the Purpose for Which I Was Created

*L*ord, I believe I was born for such a time as this, and that You have called me to pray for others. I pray for a divine visitation of Your mercy and grace upon my city _____, and my nation _____. I declare You to be Lord over these places. I know that part of my purpose on earth is to affect these places through intercession. Help me to do that. Help me to affect the world for Your glory.

The inhabitants of one city shall go to another, saying, "Let us continue to go and pray before the LORD."

ZECHARIAH 8:21

Lord, Move Me into the Purpose for Which I Was Created

⚬⚭⚬

*L*ord, give me a vision for my life. I put my identity in You and my destiny in Your hands. Show me if what I am doing now is what I am supposed to be doing. I want what You are building in my life to last for eternity. I know that all things work together for good to those who love You and are called according to Your purpose (Romans 8:28). I pray that You would show me clearly what the gifts and talents are that You have placed in me. Lead me in the way I should go as I grow in them. Enable me to use them according to Your will and for Your glory.

⚬⚭⚬

In Him also we have obtained an inheritance, being predestined according to the purpose of Him who works all things according to the counsel of His will.

EPHESIANS 1:11

Lord, Move Me into the Purpose for Which I Was Created

~~~

*L*ord, I thank You that You have a high purpose for my life. Help me to know what that purpose is. I want to do great things for You, but I know that only You can make that happen. Only Your greatness in me can accomplish great things through me. So I submit myself totally to You. I give You my life and all that I have to be used for Your glory.

~~~

May He grant you according to your heart's desire and fulfill all your purpose.

PSALM 20:4

Lord, Guide Me in All My Relationships

*L*ord, I lift up every one of my relationships to You and ask You to bless them. I ask that Your peace would reign in them and that each one would be glorifying to You. Help me to choose my friends wisely so I won't be led astray. Give me discernment and strength to separate myself from anyone who is not a good influence. I release all my relationships to You and pray that Your will be done in each one of them. I especially pray for my relationship with each of my family members. I pray You would bring healing, reconciliation, and restoration where it is needed. Bless these relationships and make them strong.

God sets the solitary in families; He brings out those who are bound into prosperity.

PSALM 68:6

Lord, Guide Me
in All My Relationships

*L*ord, I pray that You would bless my family and friends. Specifically, I lift up to You (name family members and friends). Help me to have a good relationship with each of these people. Take anyone out of my life who influences me in a way that is contrary to your will. I also lift up to You my church family and people I see in my work and throughout my day (name specific people who come to mind). Enable me to be a light to them.

Continue earnestly in prayer, being vigilant in it with thanksgiving.

COLOSSIANS 4:2

Lord, Guide Me
in All My Relationships

❧❧❧

*L*ord, I pray for any relationships I have with people who don't know You. Give me words to say that will turn their hearts toward You. Specifically, I pray for (name an unbeliever or someone who has walked away from God). Soften this person's heart to open her (his) eyes to receive You and follow You faithfully. I also pray for godly friends, role models, and mentors to come into my life. Send people who will speak the truth in love. I pray especially for people who are trustworthy, kind, loving, and faithful. Help us to be always kind, encouraging, and forgiving toward one another.

❧

Let all bitterness, wrath, anger, clamor, and evil speaking be put away from you, with all malice. And be kind to one another, tenderhearted, forgiving one another, just as God in Christ forgave you.

EPHESIANS 4:31-32

Lord, Guide Me in All My Relationships

❧

*L*ord, send people into my life with whom I can pray often. Whenever I have the opportunity to pray with others, help us to come to a place of complete unity with one another. May we always be in one accord so that our prayers are effective and powerful. Help us to submit to one another in the fear of God (Ephesians 5:21). Help us to "walk by the same rule" and "be of the same mind" (Philippians 3:16). Thank You that You will hear and answer our prayers as a result.

❧

Be of the same mind toward one another.

ROMANS 12:16

Lord, Keep Me in the Center of Your Will

*L*ord, guide my every step. Lead me in Your righteousness and make Your way straight before my face (Psalm 5:8). As I draw close and walk in intimate relationship with You each day, I pray You will get me where I need to go. Even as Jesus said, Not My will, but Yours, be done (Luke 22:42), so I say to You, not *my* will but *Your* will be done in my life. I delight to do Your will, O my God (Psalm 40:8). You are more important to me than anything. Your will is more important to me than my desires. I want to live as Your servant, doing Your will from my heart (Ephesians 6:6).

Not everyone who says to Me, "Lord, Lord," shall enter the kingdom of heaven, but he who does the will of My Father in heaven.

MATTHEW 7:21

Lord, Keep Me in the Center of Your Will

⟨∾⟩

*L*ord, give me confidence to bring all my prayers before You. Help me to trust Your willingness to hear and respond. Enable me to pray according to Your will at all times. My ultimate prayer is for Your will to be done in all things. Teach me how to pray so that I can always stay in the center of Your will.

⟨∾⟩

Now this is the confidence that we have in Him, that if we ask anything according to His will, He hears us. And if we know that He hears us, whatever we ask, we know that we have the petitions that we have asked of Him.

1 JOHN 5:14-15

Lord, Keep Me in the Center of Your Will

*L*ord, help me to hear Your voice saying, This is the way, walk in it. Speak to me from Your Word so that I will have understanding. Show me any area of my life where I am not right on target. If there is something I should be doing, reveal it to me so that I can correct my course. I want to do only what You want me to do and go only where You want me to go. I know we are not to direct our own steps (Jeremiah 10:23). I want to move into all You have for me and become all You made me to be by walking in Your perfect will for my life now.

You have need of endurance, so that after you have done the will of God, you may receive the promise.

HEBREWS 10:36

Lord, Protect Me
and All I Care About

Lord, I pray for Your hand of protection to be upon me. I trust in Your Word, which assures me that You are my rock, my fortress, my deliverer, my shield, my stronghold, and my strength in whom I trust. I want to dwell in Your secret place and abide in Your shadow (Psalm 91:1). Keep me under the umbrella of Your protection. Help me never to stray from the center of Your will or off the path You have for me. Enable me to always hear Your voice guiding me. Send Your angels to keep charge over me and keep me in all my ways. May they bear me up, so that I will not even stumble (Psalm 91:12).

Because you have made the LORD, who is my refuge, even the Most High, your dwelling place, no evil shall befall you, nor shall any plague come near your dwelling.

PSALM 91:9-10

Lord, Protect Me
and All I Care About

❧❧❧

*L*ord, You are my refuge and strength and a very present help in trouble. Therefore I will not fear, even though the earth be removed and though the mountains be carried to the midst of the sea (Psalm 46:1-2). Protect me from the plans of evil people, and keep me from sudden danger. Be merciful to me, O God, be merciful to me! For my soul trusts in You; and in the shadow of Your wings I will make my refuge (Psalm 57:1). Thank You that I will both lie down in peace, and sleep; for You alone, O Lord, make me dwell in safety (Psalm 4:8). Thank You for Your promises of protection.

❧❧❧

When you pass through the waters, I will be with you; and through the rivers, they shall not overflow you. When you walk through the fire, you shall not be burned, nor shall the flame scorch you.

ISAIAH 43:2

Lord, Give Me Wisdom to Make Right Decisions

ᘓᘏᘓᑙ

*L*ord, I pray You would give me Your wisdom and understanding in all things. I know wisdom is better than gold and understanding better than silver (Proverbs 16:16), so make me rich in wisdom and wealthy in understanding. Thank You that You give wisdom to the wise and knowledge to those who have understanding (Daniel 2:21). Increase my wisdom and knowledge so I can see Your truth in every situation. Give me discernment for each decision I must make. Please help me to always seek godly counsel and not look to the world and ungodly people for answers. Thank You, Lord, that You will give me the counsel and instruction I need, even as I sleep.

ᘓᘏᑙ

The mouth of the righteous speaks wisdom, and his tongue talks of justice. The law of his God is in his heart; none of his steps shall slide.

PSALM 37:30-31

Lord, Give Me Wisdom to Make Right Decisions

Lord, I reverence You and I look to You for everything in my life. Thank You that You will give me the counsel I need for decisions I must make. Where I should seek the counsel of others, lead me to godly people for help. I love You and Your law and Your word. Make me to be a wise person who moves in accordance with your ways.

The fear of the LORD is the beginning of wisdom.

PROVERBS 9:10

Lord, Give Me Wisdom to Make Right Decisions

Lord, You said in Your Word that You store up sound wisdom for the upright (Proverbs 2:7). Help me to walk uprightly, righteously, and obediently to Your commands. May I never be wise in my own eyes, but may I always fear You. Keep me far from evil so that I can claim the health and strength Your Word promises (Proverbs 3:7-8). Give me the wisdom, knowledge, understanding, direction, and discernment I need to keep me away from the plans of evil so that I will walk safely and not stumble (Proverbs 2:10-13). Lord, I know that in You are hidden all the treasures of wisdom and knowledge (Colossians 2:3). Help me to discover those treasures.

Through wisdom a house is built, and by understanding it is established; by knowledge the rooms are filled with all precious and pleasant riches.

PROVERBS 24:3-4

Lord, Deliver Me
from Every Evil Work

Lord, thank You that You have promised to deliver me from every evil work and preserve me for Your heavenly kingdom (2 Timothy 4:18). I know that we do not wrestle against flesh and blood, but against principalities, against powers, against the rulers of the darkness of this age, against spiritual hosts of wickedness in the heavenly places (Ephesians 6:12). Thank You that You have put all these enemies under Your feet (Ephesians 1:22), and there is nothing covered that will not be revealed, and hidden that will not be known (Matthew 10:26). My times are in Your hand; deliver me from the hand of my enemies, and from those who persecute me (Psalm 31:15).

Because he has set his love upon Me, therefore I will deliver him, I will set him on high, because he has known My name.

PSALM 91:14

Lord, Deliver Me from Every Evil Work

❧❧❧

*L*ord, I ask that You would deliver me from anything that binds me or separates me from You. I specifically ask to be delivered from (name a specific area where you want to be set free). Where I have opened the door for the enemy with my own desires, I repent of that. In Jesus' name, I pray that every stronghold erected around me by the enemy will be brought down to nothing. Make darkness light before me and the crooked places straight (Isaiah 42:16). I know that You who have begun a good work in me will complete it (Philippians 1:6). Give me patience to not give up and the strength to stand strong in Your Word.

❧❧❧

Call upon Me in the day of trouble; I will deliver you, and you shall glorify Me.

PSALM 50:15

Lord, Set Me Free
from Negative Emotions

*L*ord, help me to live in Your joy and peace. Give me strength and understanding to resist anxiety, anger, envy, depression, bitterness, hopelessness, loneliness, fear, and guilt. Rescue me when my spirit is overwhelmed within me; my heart within me is distressed (Psalm 143:4). I refuse to let my life be brought down by negative emotions such as these. When I am tempted to give in to them, show me Your truth. You have said in Your Word that by our patience we can possess our souls (Luke 21:19). Give me patience so I can do that. Help me to keep my heart with all diligence, for I know that out of it spring the issues of life (Proverbs 4:23).

*The righteous cry out, and the L*ORD *hears, and delivers them out of all their troubles. The L*ORD *is near to those who have a broken heart, and saves such as have a contrite spirit.*

PSALM 34:17-18

Lord, Set Me Free
from Negative Emotions

*L*ord, help me to not be insecure and self-focused so that I miss opportunities to focus on You and extend Your love. May I be sensitive to the needs, trials, and weaknesses of others and not overly sensitive to myself. What You accomplished on the cross is my source of greatest joy. Help me to concentrate on that. Thank You, Lord, that in my distress I can call on You. Cause me to hear Your lovingkindness in the morning, for in You do I trust; cause me to know the way in which I should walk, for I lift up my soul to You (Psalm 143:8). May the joy of knowing You fill my heart with happiness and peace.

> *Be anxious for nothing, but in everything by prayer and supplication, with thanksgiving, let your requests be made known to God; and the peace of God, which surpasses all understanding, will guard your hearts and minds through Christ Jesus.*

PHILIPPIANS 4:6-7

Lord, Comfort Me in Times of Trouble

⨳

*L*ord, help me remember that no matter how dark my situation may become, You are the light of my life and can never be put out. No matter what dark clouds settle on my life, You will lift me above the storm and into the comfort of Your presence. Only You can take whatever loss I experience and fill that empty place with good. Only You can take away my grief and pain and dry my tears. Hear me when I call, O God of my righteousness! You have relieved me in my distress; have mercy on me, and hear my prayer (Psalm 4:1). I want to stand strong in Your truth and not be swept away by my emotions.

⨳

Blessed are the poor in spirit, for theirs is the kingdom of heaven. Blessed are those who mourn, for they shall be comforted.

MATTHEW 5:3-4

Lord, Comfort Me in Times of Trouble

*L*ord, help me remember to give thanks to You in all things, knowing that You reign in the midst of them. I know when I pass through the waters You will be with me and the river will not overflow me. When I walk through the fire I will not be burned, nor will the flame touch me (Isaiah 43:1-2). I pray that You, O God of hope, will fill me with all joy and peace and faith so that I will abound in hope by the power of the Holy Spirit (Romans 15:13). Thank You that You have sent Your Holy Spirit to be my Comforter and Helper. Please remind me of that in the midst of difficult times.

May the God of all grace, who called us to His eternal glory by Christ Jesus, after you have suffered a while, perfect, establish, strengthen, and settle you.

1 PETER 5:10

Lord, Enable Me to Resist the Temptation to Sin

*L*ord, do not allow me to be led into temptation, but deliver me from the evil one and his plans for my downfall. In the name of Jesus, I break any hold temptation has on me. Keep me strong and able to resist anything that would tempt me away from all You have for me. I pray I will have no secret thoughts where I entertain ungodly desires to do or say something I shouldn't. I pray that I will have no secret life where I do things I would be ashamed to have others see. I don't want to have fellowship with unfruitful works of darkness. Help me, instead, to expose them (Ephesians 5:11).

Blessed is the man who endures temptation; for when he has been approved, he will receive the crown of life which the Lord has promised to those who love Him.

JAMES 1:12

Lord, Enable Me to Resist the Temptation to Sin

*L*ord, help me to hide Your Word in my heart so I will see clearly and not sin against You in any way (Psalm 119:11). Thank You, Lord, that You are near to all who call upon You, and You will fulfill the desire of those who fear You. Thank You that You hear my cries and will save me from any weakness that could lead me away from all You have for me (Psalm 145:18-19). Thank You that You know how to deliver the godly out of temptations (2 Peter 2:9). Thank You that You will deliver me out of all temptation and keep it far from me.

No temptation has overtaken you except such as is common to man; but God is faithful, who will not allow you to be tempted beyond what you are able, but with the temptation will also make the way of escape, that you may be able to bear it.

1 CORINTHIANS 10:13

Lord, Heal Me and Help Me Care for My Body

*L*ord, I thank You that You are the Healer. I look to You for my healing whenever I am injured or sick. I pray that You would strengthen and heal me today. Specifically, I pray for (name any area where you need the Lord to heal you). Heal me that it might be fulfilled which was spoken by Isaiah the prophet, saying: He Himself took our infirmities and bore our sicknesses (Matthew 8:17). You suffered, died, and were buried for me so that I might have healing, forgiveness, and eternal life. By Your stripes, I am healed (1 Peter 2:24). In Your presence I can reach out and touch You and in turn be touched by You.

Heal me, O Lord, and I shall be healed; save me, and I shall be saved, for You are my praise.

JEREMIAH 17:14

Lord, Heal Me and Help Me Care for My Body

❧❧❧

*L*ord, I present my body to You as a living sacrifice, holy and acceptable (Romans 12:1). Teach me how to treat it with care and be a good steward of it. Help me not to mistreat it in any way or use it improperly. Teach me Your ways so that I will not violate the way You want me to take care of my body, which is the temple of Your Holy Spirit.

❧❧

You were bought at a price; therefore glorify God in your body and in your spirit, which are God's.

1 CORINTHIANS 6:20

Lord, Heal Me and Help Me Care for My Body

*L*ord, I want everything I do to be glorifying to You. Help me to be a good steward of the body You have given me. Teach me and help me learn. Lead me to people who can help or advise me. When I am sick and need to see a doctor, show me which doctor to see and give that doctor wisdom as to how to treat me. Enable me to discipline my body and bring it into subjection (1 Corinthians 9:27). Help me to always remember and fully understand that my body is the temple of Your Holy Spirit, who dwells in me, so that I can make choices that keep my temple clean, healthy, and protected.

Therefore, whether you eat or drink, or whatever you do, do all to the glory of God.

1 CORINTHIANS 10:31

Lord, Heal Me and Help Me Care for My Body

*L*ord, enable me to make good decisions with regard to maintaining healthful habits. Thank You that You are my healer. Specifically I pray for (name any area where you need the Lord to help you or heal you). Help me to find healing through Your Word, through prayer, and through faith in You as my healer. Thank You that You love us so much.

He sent His word and healed them.

PSALM 107:20

Lord, Free Me from Ungodly Fear

✦

*L*ord, You are my light and my salvation. You are the strength of my life. Of whom, then, shall I be afraid? (Psalm 27:1). I will be strong and of good courage, for I know You are with me wherever I go (Joshua 1:9). Free me from all ungodly fear, for I know fear is never of You. I pray You would guard my heart and mind from the spirit of fear. If I experience feelings of fear, I pray You would replace them with Your perfect love. If I have gotten my mind off of You and on my circumstances, help me to reverse that process so that my mind is off my circumstances and on You.

✦

God has not given us a spirit of fear, but of power and of love and of a sound mind.

2 TIMOTHY 1:7

Lord, Free Me
from Ungodly Fear

*L*ord, I know that You have not given me a spirit of fear, so I reject that and instead claim the power, love, and sound mind You have for me. Oh, how great is Your goodness, which You have laid up for those who fear You (Psalm 31:19). Because I have received a kingdom that cannot be shaken, may I have grace by which to serve You acceptably with reverence and godly fear all the days of my life (Hebrews 12:28). Help me to know Your Word so well that I will reject fear the moment it enters my mind and soul.

Teach me Your way, O LORD; I will walk in Your truth; unite my heart to fear Your name.

PSALM 86:11

Lord, Use Me to Touch the Lives of Others

*L*ord, help me to serve You the way You want me to. Reveal to me any area of my life where I should be giving to someone right now. Open my eyes to see the need. Give me a generous heart to give to the poor. Help me to be a good steward of the blessings You have given me by sharing what I have with others. Show me whom You want me to extend my hand to at this time. Fill me with Your love for all people, and help me to communicate it in a way that can be clearly perceived. Use me to touch the lives of others with the hope that is in me.

By this we know love, because He laid down His life for us. And we also ought to lay down our lives for the brethren.

1 JOHN 3:16

Lord, Use Me to Touch the Lives of Others

ᗺᗷᗷᗸᗷᗷᗸ

*L*ord, You have said that when just two people are gathered in Your name, You are there in the midst of them (Matthew 18:20). What a wonderful promise to us. You have also said that when two of us *agree* in prayer, You will answer (Matthew 18:19). I pray You will help me to find someone with whom I can agree. Lead me to people for whom and with whom I can pray. Thank You in advance for the answers to those prayers of agreement.

ᗺᗷᗸ

If two of you agree on earth concerning anything that they ask, it will be done for them by My Father in heaven.

MATTHEW 18:19

Lord, Use Me to Touch the Lives of Others

❧

*L*ord, show me what You want me to do today to be a blessing to others. I don't want to get so wrapped up in my own life that I don't see the opportunity for ministering Your life to those around me. Show me what You want me to do and enable me to do it. Give me all I need to minister life, hope, help, and healing to others. Make me to be one of Your faithful intercessors, and teach me how to pray in power. Help me to make a big difference in the world because You are working through me to touch lives for Your glory. May my greatest treasure always be in serving You.

❧

As each one has received a gift, minister it to one another, as good stewards of the manifold grace of God.

1 PETER 4:10

Lord, Use Me to Touch the Lives of Others

～✦～

*L*ord, show me how I can be a conduit of Your love for others. Help me to show Your love in prayer. Work through me when I pray with another person so that I will pray right on target. Help me to hear Your Holy Spirit leading me and giving me knowledge, revelation, and discernment. Make me into a powerful prayer warrior, and an instrument of Your healing love.

～✦～

And this I pray, that your love may abound still more and more in knowledge and all discernment.

PHILIPPIANS 1:9

Lord, Train Me to Speak Only Words That Bring Life

$\mathcal{L}$ord, help me be a person who speaks words that build up and not tear down. Help me to speak life into the situations and people around me, and not death. Fill my heart afresh each day with Your Holy Spirit so that Your love and goodness overflow from my heart and my mouth. Holy Spirit of truth, guide me in all truth. Let the words of my mouth and the meditation of my heart be acceptable in Your sight, O Lord, my strength and my Redeemer (Psalm 19:14). May every word I speak reflect Your purity and love.

Righteous lips are the delight of kings, and they love him who speaks what is right.

PROVERBS 16:13

Lord, Train Me to Speak Only Words That Bring Life

*L*ord, help me to speak only words that are true, noble, just, pure, lovely, of good report, virtuous, excellent, or praiseworthy (Philippians 4:8). Help me to always be able to give the reason for the hope that is within me (1 Peter 3:15). Help me to speak the truth in love (Ephesians 4:15). Fill me with Your love so that it flows from me in the words I speak. May every word I speak bring life and encouragement and positive reinforcement to all who hear me. Help me to speak of Your goodness to everyone.

My tongue shall speak of Your righteousness and of Your praise all the day long.

PSALM 35:28

Lord, Train Me to Speak Only Words That Bring Life

*L*ord, Your Word says that the preparations of the heart belong to man, but the answer of the tongue is from the Lord (Proverbs 16:1). I will prepare my heart by being in Your Word every day and obeying Your laws. I will prepare my heart by worshiping You and giving thanks in all things. Fill my heart with love, peace, and joy so that it will flow from my mouth. I pray You would give me the words to say every time I speak. Show me when to speak and when not to. And when I do speak, give me words to say that will bring life and edification and comfort.

Pleasant words are like a honeycomb, sweetness to the soul and health to the bones.

PROVERBS 16:24

Lord, Transform Me into a Woman of Mountain-Moving Faith

*L*ord, increase my faith. Teach me how to walk by faith, not by sight (2 Corinthians 5:7). Give me strength to stand strong on Your promises and believe Your every word. I know that faith comes by hearing, and hearing by the word of God (Romans 10:17). Make my faith increase every time I hear or read Your Word. Increase my faith so that I can pray in power. Help me to believe for Your promises to be fulfilled in me. I pray that the genuineness of my faith, which is more precious than gold that perishes even when it is tested by fire, will be glorifying to You, Lord (1 Peter 1:7).

If you have faith as a mustard seed, you will say to this mountain, Move from here to there, and it will move; and nothing will be impossible for you.

MATTHEW 17:20

Lord, Transform Me into a Woman of Mountain-Moving Faith

❦

*L*ord, grow me up in knowledge of the power of prayer. As I reach out to pray with and for others, give me ever-increasing faith to believe for the answers. I know that with You, God, nothing is impossible. Your Word not only says that, but illustrates it time and again. Help me to have faith strong enough to move the mountains in my life.

❦

Whatever things you ask in prayer, believing, you will receive.

MATTHEW 21:22

Lord, Transform Me into a Woman of Mountain-Moving Faith

*L*ord, I know faith is the substance of things hoped for, the evidence of things not seen (Hebrews 11:1). I know I have been saved through faith, and it is a gift from You (Ephesians 2:8). Help me to take the shield of faith to quench all the fiery darts of the wicked one (Ephesians 6:16). I know that whatever is not from faith is sin (Romans 14:23). I confess any doubt I have as sin before You, and I ask You to forgive me. I don't want to hinder what You want to do in me and through me because of doubt. Increase my faith daily so that I can pray in Your name and see powerful things happen.

Having been justified by faith, we have peace with God through our Lord Jesus Christ.

ROMANS 5:1

Lord, Transform Me into a Woman of Mountain-Moving Faith

*L*ord, I want to always pray with Your clear leading and guidance. When I pray, give me great faith to believe for the answers. I know that without faith it is impossible to please You (Hebrews 11:6), and I want to please You more than anything else. I believe that You hear my prayers and will answer. I believe that there is a great reward for those who seek You with all their heart.

Without faith it is impossible to please Him, for he who comes to God must believe that He is, and that He is a rewarder of those who diligently seek Him.

HEBREWS 11:6

Lord, Change Me
into the Likeness of Christ

*L*ord, I want to be changed, and I pray those changes will begin today. I know I can't change myself in any way that is significant or lasting, but by the transforming power of Your Holy Spirit all things are possible. Grant me, according to the riches of Your glory, to be strengthened with might through Your Spirit in my inner being (Ephesians 3:16). I know that You will supply all that I need according to Your riches in Christ Jesus (Philippians 4:19). Help me to become separate from the world without becoming isolated from it. May Your love manifested in me be a witness of Your greatness.

I have been crucified with Christ; it is no longer I who live, but Christ lives in me; and the life which I now live in the flesh I live by faith in the Son of God, who loved me and gave Himself for me.

GALATIANS 2:20

Lord, Change Me
into the Likeness of Christ

$\mathcal{L}$ord, teach me to love others the way You do. Soften my heart where it has become hard. Make me fresh where I have become stale. Lead me and instruct me where I have become unteachable. Make me to be faithful, giving, and obedient the way Jesus was. Where I am resistant to change, help me to trust Your work in my life. May Your light so shine in me that I become a light to all who know me. May it be not I who lives, but You who lives in me (Galatians 2:20). Make me to be so much like Christ that when people see me they will want to know You better.

The Spirit Himself bears witness with our spirit that we are children of God, and if children, then heirs—heirs of God and joint heirs with Christ.

ROMANS 8:16-17

Lord, Lift Me out of My Past

*L*ord, I pray that You would set me free from my past. Wherever I have made the past my home, I pray that You would deliver me, heal me, and redeem me from it. Help me to let go of anything I have held onto of my past that has kept me from moving into all You have for me. Enable me to put off all former ways of thinking and feeling and remembering (Ephesians 4:22-24). Give me the mind of Christ so I will be able to understand when I am being controlled by memories of past events. I release my past to You and everyone associated with it so You can restore what has been lost.

If anyone is in Christ, he is a new creation; old things have passed away; behold all things have become new.

2 CORINTHIANS 5:17

Lord, Lift Me
out of My Past

*L*ord, make me glad according to the days in which I have been afflicted and the years I have seen evil (Psalm 90:15). Thank You that You make all things new and You are making me new in every way (Revelation 21:5). Help me to keep my eyes looking straight ahead and to forgive what needs to be forgiven. I know You want to do something new in my life today. Help me to concentrate on where I am to go now and not where I have been. Release me from the past so I can move out of it and into the future You have for me.

Do not remember the former things, nor consider the things of old. Behold, I will do a new thing, now it shall spring forth; shall you not know it? I will even make a road in the wilderness and rivers in the desert.

ISAIAH 43:18-19

Lord, Lead Me into the Future You Have for Me

*L*ord, I put my future in Your hands and ask that You would give me total peace about it. I want to be in the center of Your plans for my life, knowing You have given me everything I need for what is ahead. I pray You would give me strength to endure without giving up. You have said that he who endures to the end will be saved (Matthew 10:22). Help me to run the race in a way that I shall finish strong and receive the prize You have for me (1 Corinthians 9:24). Help me to be always watchful in my prayers, because I don't know when the end of my life will be (1 Peter 4:7).

But the path of the just is like the shining sun, that shines ever brighter unto the perfect day.

PROVERBS 4:18

PART II

The Prayer *That* CHANGES EVERYTHING

Because He Is
My Creator

O Lord, thank You that You created me and gave me life. You formed my inward parts; You covered me in my mother's womb (Psalm 139:13). I praise You, for I am fearfully and wonderfully made; marvelous are Your works, and that my soul knows very well (Psalm 139:14). I praise You that I was created for good things. Help me to be renewed in the image of You, my Creator (Colossians 3:10 NIV). I know You made me to be so much more than I am now and that You will help me become all You created me to be. Thank You, Jesus, that You are the image of the invisible God, the firstborn over all creation (Colossians 1:15).

Christ himself is the Creator who made every-thing in heaven and earth, the things we can see and the things we can't; the spirit world with its kings and kingdoms, its rulers and authorities; all were made by Christ for his own use and glory.

COLOSSIANS 1:16 TLB

Because He Is My Creator

*L*ord, I worship You as the Creator of heaven and earth. All things were made by You and everything You created is good. I praise You for all of Your beautiful creation. You placed the earth on its foundation so that it can never be moved (Psalm 104:5). Your right hand stretched out the heavens (Isaiah 48:13). Thank You that You have blessed us with light and dark, sun and rain, food and water, land and sea, trees and flowers, days and seasons. The heavens are Yours, the earth also is Yours; the world and all its fullness, You have founded them (Psalm 89:11). How many are your works, O Lord! In wisdom you have made them all; the earth is full of your creatures (Psalm 104:24 niv).

Be exalted, O God, above the heavens; let Your glory be above all the earth.

PSALM 57:11

Because He Is
My Heavenly Father

*H*eavenly Father, I worship You this day. You are closer to me than an earthly father ever could be. Thank You that as my Father, You care about what happens to me. You provide for me, teach me, plan for my future, supply all my needs, and, because You love me, You will never let me get away with disobedience to Your rules. Thank You that You have given me the heritage of those who fear Your name, and I have inherited great and eternal riches from You (Psalm 61:5). Lord, you alone are my inheritance, my cup of blessing. You guard all that is mine. The land you have given me is a pleasant land. What a wonderful inheritance! (Psalm 16:5-6 NLT).

Your Father knows the things you have need of before you ask Him.

MATTHEW 6:8

Because He Is
My Heavenly Father

❦

*L*ord, help me to forgive my earthly father for anything he did or did not do. Show me if there is anything I have not forgiven that I am not seeing. As Your child, I long to make You proud. Help me to always do what is pleasing in Your sight. I want to be separate from all that would keep me separated from You (2 Corinthians 6:17-18). Thank You that I have been predestined to be adopted as Your child through Jesus because it gives You pleasure and it is Your will for my life (Ephesians 1:5). I praise and honor You as my Father God and give thanks always for all things, especially Your love (Ephesians 5:20).

❦

Seek the kingdom of God, and all these things shall be added to you. Do not fear, little flock, for it is your Father's good pleasure to give you the kingdom.

LUKE 12:31-32

Because He Loves Me

*L*ord, it is amazing that You love me so, even though I have done nothing to deserve it. What is man, that You should exalt him, that You should set Your heart on him? (Job 7:17). Thank You that You see my ways and count all my steps (Job 31:4). Thank You that Your favor is for life (Psalm 30:5). O Lord, because Your lovingkindness is better than life, my lips shall praise You. Thus I will bless You while I live; I will lift up my hands in Your name (Psalm 63:3-4). I love You with all my heart, mind, and soul, and I worship You as my God of love.

Can a woman forget her nursing child, and not have compassion on the son of her womb? Surely they may forget, yet I will not forget you. See, I have inscribed you on the palms of My hands.

ISAIAH 49:15-16

Because He Loves Me

*L*ord, I worship You and thank You that You are the God of love. Thank You for loving me before I even knew You. I praise You especially for sacrificing Your only Son for me. There is no greater love than that. Your love brings healing to me for all the times and ways I have felt unloved in my life. I know that no matter what is happening in my life or what *will* happen in my life, Your love for me will never end. Because of Your love, I will praise You, O Lord, with my whole heart; I will tell of all Your marvelous works. I will be glad and rejoice in You; I will sing praise to Your name, O Most High (Psalm 9:1-2).

In this is love, not that we loved God, but that He loved us and sent His Son to be the propitiation for our sins.

1 JOHN 4:10

Because He Laid Down His Life for Me

*L*ord, I worship You and thank You that even before the creation of the world You chose me to be holy and blameless in Your sight. Thank You that because of Your great love, You predestined me to be adopted as Your child through Jesus in accordance with Your will. Thank You, Jesus, that because of You I have been redeemed through the shedding of Your blood. Lord, I know that I have sinned and fall far short of Your glory (Romans 3:23). Thank You for forgiving me. Thank You that even though I was dead in sin, You have made me alive in Christ (Ephesians 2:4-5). Thank You for the richness of Your mercy and grace which You have lavished on me.

For God so loved the world that He gave His only begotten Son, that whoever believes in Him should not perish but have everlasting life.

JOHN 3:16

Because He Laid Down His Life for Me

*L*ord, thank You for sending Your Son, Jesus, to be my Savior and Redeemer. Praise You, Jesus, for the price You paid, the sacrifice You made, and the unthinkable suffering and death You willingly endured on the cross for me. Because of You, I am forgiven and now have made peace with my Creator. Thank You for giving me new birth into a life of hope because of Your resurrection. You enlarged my path under me; so my feet did not slip (2 Samuel 22:36-37). Lord, I thank You that I have been saved and reconciled to You because of Your Son, Jesus (Romans 5:10-11).

Blessed be the God and Father of our Lord Jesus Christ, who according to His abundant mercy has begotten us again to a living hope through the resurrection of Jesus Christ from the dead, to an inheritance incorruptible and undefiled and that does not fade away, reserved in heaven for you.

1 PETER 1:3-4

Because He
Has Forgiven Me

*L*ord, thank You that You are continually willing to forgive me and mold me into a whole person. Thank You for convicting me of my sins so that I can come humbly before You and confess them. Thank You that no matter how far I stray from Your ways, You will always receive me back when I repent and cry out to You for forgiveness. Forgive me for my sins today. Remind me whenever I stray from Your laws so that I can confess and repent and receive Your forgiveness. I don't want any sin of mine to come between us. Cleanse me of all that is not of You. I worship You, O Lord, my Forgiver and Redeemer.

If we confess our sins, He is faithful and just to forgive us our sins and to cleanse us from all unrighteousness.

1 JOHN 1:9

Because He Has Forgiven Me

*L*ord, You are the keeper of my heart and the forgiver of my soul. I praise You for sending Your Son to die for me so that I could be forgiven. Thank You that You forgive my wickedness and will remember my sins no more (Hebrews 8:12 NIV). I know that I was dead in sins, but You, O God, have made me alive in Christ and have forgiven me of everything (Colossians 2:13). I am grateful that there is no condemnation for those of us who walk with Jesus (Romans 8:1). Thank You that the law of the Spirit of life has set me free from the law of sin and death (Romans 8:2). I praise You as my Lord and wonderful God of forgiveness.

Create in me a clean heart, O God, and renew a steadfast spirit within me.

PSALM 51:10

Because He Has Given Me His Holy Spirit

*L*ord, fill me afresh with Your Spirit this day. I let go of all else and open my life to all of You. Enable me to resist the temptations of the flesh that would cause me to stray from the path You have for me. I don't ever want to minimize all that You want to do in my life. Help me to be ever mindful of Your presence in me, and may I always hear Your clear leading. I want to show my love for You by embracing You with my worship and touching You with my praise. Teach me all I need to know about how to worship You in ways that are pleasing in Your sight.

I will pray the Father, and He will give you another Helper, that He may abide with you forever.

JOHN 14:16

Because He Has Given Me His Holy Spirit

*L*ord, I worship You and praise You and thank You for Your Holy Spirit in my life. Thank You, Jesus, for sending me the Comforter and Helper to teach and guide me every day. I praise You for the wisdom, revelation, and knowledge that You impart to me. I love You and the joy You bring into my life (1 Thessalonians 1:6). Thank You that I have been sealed with the Holy Spirit of promise (Ephesians 1:13). I know that I cannot understand the things of God in my flesh, but I can discern them in my spirit because of You dwelling in me. Thank You, Lord, for the gift of Your Holy Spirit in me.

Now hope does not disappoint, because the love of God has been poured out in our hearts by the Holy Spirit who was given to us.

ROMANS 5:5

Because He Gave Me His Word

*L*ord, Your Word changes my heart, enriches my soul, and makes me wise. All Your commandments are true, right, pure, dependable, edifying, and life-giving, and that makes me glad. They instruct me, and I find great peace when I obey them (Psalm 19:7-11). Help me to hold fast the word of life, so that I may rejoice in the day of Christ that I have not run in vain or labored in vain (Philippians 2:16). I will worship toward Your holy temple, and praise Your name for Your loving-kindness and Your truth; for You have magnified Your word above all Your name (Psalm 138:2). Thank You that Your Word will stand forever because You, Lord, are the Living Word who always was and forever will be.

The law of the LORD is perfect, converting the soul; the testimony of the LORD is sure, making wise the simple.

PSALM 19:7

Because He Gave
Me His Word

*L*ord, raise up an army of prayer warriors who can be mobilized on a moment's notice so that we can move in unity and by the power of Your Spirit. Help us to understand the powerful weapon we have in Your Word as we move into battle in prayer. If *You* are for us, who can be against us (Romans 8:31)? Thank You, Lord, that I can always depend upon Your Word to be the ultimate truth for my life.

For the weapons of our warfare are not carnal but mighty in God for pulling down strongholds.

2 CORINTHIANS 10:4

Because He Gave
Me His Word

*L*ord, I praise and thank You for Your Word. How I love that it gives me the guidance I need for my life. My delight is in Your law. Help me to meditate on it day and night (Psalm 1:2). Your testimonies also are my delight and my counselors (Psalm 119:24). Help me to fully understand all that I read in Your Word. Reveal everything I need to know. Open my eyes, that I may see wondrous things from Your law (Psalm 119:18). Thank You that every time I read Your Word, I know You better. Your Word is a love letter to me, showing me how much You love me. And every time I read it, I love You more.

Great peace have those who love Your law, and nothing causes them to stumble.

PSALM 119:165

Because He Is
a Good God

*L*ord, help me to trust that You are a good God no matter what is going on in my life. Help me to believe without any doubting that even if bad things are happening, Your goodness will reign in the midst of them all. Thank You that Your plans for me are for good. Thank You that the future You have for me is good. Thank You that You bring good things into my life. Reveal Your goodness to me more and more so that I may praise You for it. How great is Your goodness to those who trust and fear You (Psalm 31:19). O Lord, how excellent is Your name in all the earth (Psalm 8:1).

Oh, that men would give thanks to the LORD for His goodness, and for His wonderful works to the children of men!

PSALM 107:8

Because He Is a Good God

*L*ord, I know that even when I go through bad or difficult times, You are good. I know that nothing is good outside of You. Help me to trust Your goodness no matter what I see going on in my life or in situations around me. Thank You for Your goodness in my life every day.

I know that You are a gracious and merciful God,
slow to anger and abundant in lovingkindness,
One who relents from doing harm.

JONAH 4:2

Because He Is
a Good God

Lord, I praise You for Your greatness and Your goodness. Thank You that You are a good God and Your mercy and grace toward me will endure forever (Psalm 118:1). May I never forget all the good You have done for me and how You have filled my life with good things. I desire, as David did, that I may dwell in Your house all the days of my life, to behold Your beauty and to be in Your temple (Psalm 27:4). I bless Your name, for You are good. Your mercy is everlasting, and Your truth endures to all generations (Psalm 100:4-5). You are my God and Lord, You are loving and patient, and You abound in goodness and truth (Exodus 34:6).

The LORD is good to those who wait for Him, to the soul who seeks Him.

LAMENTATIONS 3:25

Because He Is
a Good God

*L*ord, pour out Your Spirit upon this nation. Bring unbelievers to a saving knowledge of Your Son, Jesus. Prosper us and rain Your blessings upon us, even though I know as a nation we don't deserve it. It is Your goodness that keeps us from getting what we *do* deserve. Thank You that Your eyes are on the righteous, and Your ears are open to our prayers (1 Peter 3:12). May Your love and peace so rise in our hearts that it becomes our greatest testimony of Your goodness.

Surely His salvation is near to those who fear Him, that glory may dwell in our land.

PSALM 85:9

Because
He Is Holy

*L*ord, help me to be holy as You are holy. Establish my heart holy and blameless before You (Colossians 1:22). You who are mighty have done great things for me; holy is Your name (Luke 1:49). I exalt Your holy name above all names and will give praise and thanks to You every time I think of it (Psalm 30:4). Who does not reverence You, Lord, and glorify Your name? For only You are holy (Revelation 15:4). I give You the glory due Your name, and I worship You in the beauty of Your holiness (Psalm 29:2). O Lord, You are my God. I will exalt You, and I will praise Your name, for You have done wonderful things (Isaiah 25:1).

Let them praise Your great and awesome name. He is holy. Exalt the Lord our God, and worship at His footstool. He is holy.

PSALM 99:3,5

Because
He Is Holy

Holy, holy, holy are You, Lord, and worthy to be praised. I worship You and thank You that You are perfect and lovely and pure and wonderful. The beauty of Your holiness is awesome beyond words. Thank You for wanting to impart Your holiness to me. Lord, I need Your holiness to penetrate my life and wash away anything that is unholy in me. Take away any attitude, any hidden sin of the mind, any activity or action that I do which is not what You would have for me. I know You did not call me to uncleanness, but to holiness (1 Thessalonians 4:7). Show me the way to holiness in my own life.

Give unto the LORD the glory due to His name;
worship the LORD in the beauty of holiness.

PSALM 29:2

Because He Is All-Powerful

*L*ord, You have said in Your Word that power belongs to You (Psalm 62:11). Yours, O LORD, is the greatness, the power and the glory, the victory and the majesty; for all that is in heaven and in earth is Yours (1 Chronicles 29:11). I know that by the power of Your Spirit, all things are possible. I give You thanks, O Lord God Almighty, the One who is and who was and who is to come, because You have taken Your great power and reigned (Revelation 11:17). Be exalted, O LORD, in Your own strength! (Psalm 21:13). I praise and exalt You as the all-powerful Lord of my life. Yours is the kingdom and the power and the glory forever (Matthew 6:13).

Your faith should not be in the wisdom of men but in the power of God.

1 CORINTHIANS 2:5

Because He Is All-Powerful

*L*ord, show us Your ways. Teach us Your paths. Lead us in Your truth and teach us, for You are the God of our salvation (Psalm 25:4-5). There is nothing that is too difficult for You, therefore I ask that You would enable the countries of the earth to come together and cooperate peacefully. Specifically, I pray for (name any countries where there is war or civil strife). Bring peace to these nations and people. Bless our troops with protection and favor in whatever nation they are in.

God be merciful to us and bless us, And cause His face to shine upon us, that Your way may be known on earth, Your salvation among all nations.

PSALM 67:1-2

Because He Is All-Powerful

*L*ord, I praise Your holy name this day. You are Almighty God. You are the all-powerful, omnipotent Lord of heaven and earth. There is nothing too hard for You. Great are You, Lord, and mighty in power; Your understanding is infinite (Psalm 147:5). I know that because You can do anything, no plan or purpose of Yours for my life can be held back. You have a mighty arm (Psalm 89:13), and You rule by Your power (Psalm 65:6). You are the potter and I am the clay (Isaiah 64:8), and I give You full power over my life to mold me as You see fit. I surrender my life to You and release it into Your hands.

Behold, I am the Lord, the God of all flesh. Is there anything too hard for Me?

JEREMIAH 32:27

Because He Is
with Me

*L*ord, You are all I desire. Just being with You changes everything in me. Longing for You makes me long to be free of anything that would draw my attention away. I draw close to You this day. Thank You that You promise to draw close to me. With You I am never alone. I love Your holiness, Lord. I love Your beauty. With joy I draw water from the wells of Your salvation (Isaiah 12:3). Help me to make You the first place I run to when I have longings in my heart. I don't want to waste time turning to other things that will never satisfy the need I have for intimacy with You. My soul waits for You, Lord (Psalm 33:20).

I have loved you with an everlasting love; therefore with lovingkindness I have drawn you.

JEREMIAH 31:3

Because He Is with Me

O Lord, I worship You and praise You as Immanuel, my God who is with me. I long for more of You. I seek after You and thirst for You like water in a dry land. I want to stand under the gentle waterfall of Your Spirit and feel the soothing mist of Your love showering over me. I want to be immersed in the center of the flow of Your Spirit. I want to be close enough to You to feel Your heartbeat. You are the only answer to the emptiness I feel when I am not with You. The fullness of Your being is what I crave. The intimacy of Your embrace is what I long for.

Behold, the virgin shall be with child, and bear a Son, and they shall call His name Immanuel, which is translated God with us.

MATTHEW 1:23

Because He Has a Purpose for My Life

*L*ord, I pray that You will reveal to me what I am to do and enable me to do it well. I don't want my own dreams and plans for the future to get in the way of what *You* have for me (Ecclesiastes 5:7). I know You desire mercy and knowing You more than sacrifice (Hosea 6:6). I long to know You more and to conform to the image of Your Son. May Your goodness, holiness, and beauty be upon me and establish the work of my hands (Psalm 90:17). Move me into the future You have for me as I walk in Your presence each day. Thank You that You created me with a purpose, and every time I worship You, I am fulfilling that purpose.

For we are His workmanship, created in Christ Jesus for good works, which God prepared beforehand that we should walk in them.

EPHESIANS 2:10

Because He Has a Purpose for My Life

ᕦᕤ

Heavenly Father, I worship You as my Lord and King. I praise You that You are all-knowing and can see the end from the beginning. That You uphold all things by Your power. That You hold my life in Your hand. That You see my past and my future. I lift up to You all that I am and offer my life to You. Make me an instrument through which Your will is accomplished on earth. Use what I have for Your glory. Lift me up to see things from Your perspective, and help me to rise above my limitations. I don't want to limit what You can do *in* me and *through* me because I don't have an adequate vision of what Your heart desires to accomplish.

ᕦᕤ

Therefore we also pray always for you that our God would count you worthy of this calling, and fulfill all the good pleasure of His goodness and the work of faith with power.

2 THESSALONIANS 1:11

Because He
Redeems All Things

*L*ord, I thank You for all the times You have redeemed my life from destruction. For all the times You have shown Your lovingkindness and tender mercies to me (Psalm 103:1-5). Everything in me blesses Your holy name, for You are the Lord, my Redeemer, who has made all things and made my life to be a testament to Your glory and redemption. You, O Lord, are my Father; my Redeemer from everlasting is Your name (Isaiah 63:16). Let the words of my mouth and the meditation of my heart be acceptable in Your sight, O LORD, my strength and my Redeemer (Psalm 19:14). I pray that You will continue to redeem my life in ways I never dreamed possible.

I know that my Redeemer lives.

JOB 19:25

Because He
Redeems All Things

$\mathcal{L}$ord, I thank You that You are the God of redemption and restoration. Thank You that You are all about taking the imperfect and injecting Your perfection into it. Help me to remember that so I don't give up on situations, relationships, hopes, or dreams just because I think they are unredeemable. Thank You that You love me enough to be my Redeemer.

Is My hand shortened that it cannot redeem?

ISAIAH 50:2

Because He Redeems All Things

*L*ord, I worship You as my God and Savior. I praise You, Jesus, as my precious Redeemer. Thank You for redeeming my soul from the pit of hell. Thank You for redeeming me from death (Hosea 13:14) and from the power of the grave (Psalm 49:15). Thank You for redeeming my life from oppression (Psalm 72:14). Thank You for love so great that You desire to restore my life in every way. Redeem me and revive me according to Your Word (Psalm 119:154). Thank You for Your goodness and mercy. Draw near to my soul, and redeem it (Psalm 69:18). Redeem me and be merciful to me (Psalm 26:11). Thank You for all the redemption You have already worked in my life.

The LORD redeems the soul of His servants, and none of those who trust in Him shall be condemned.

PSALM 34:22

Because He
Redeems All Things

*L*ord, I thank You that You love me so much that You want to totally restore, repair, rebuild, renew, and redeem my soul and my life. I know that no matter what damage has occurred in my life, or what loss I have experienced, there is nothing so great that You cannot redeem and restore it in some way.

The LORD redeems the soul of His servants, and none of those who trust in Him shall be condemned.

PSALM 34:22

Because He Is
the Light of the World

*L*ord, thank You that I don't have to fear the darkness because even in dark times You are there. I know that if one walks in the night, he stumbles, because the light is not in him (John 11:10). But Your light is in me, Jesus, because You have come as a light into the world so that I don't have to live in darkness (John 12:46). The enemy wants me to dwell in darkness, but You have given me light. I choose to walk in that light. I need no other light but Yours. Whatever is good and perfect comes from You, the Creator of all light, and You will shine forever without change (James 1:17 TLB).

Arise, shine; for your light has come! And the glory of the LORD is risen upon you. For behold, the darkness shall cover the earth, and deep darkness the people; but the LORD will arise over you, and His glory will be seen upon you.

ISAIAH 60:1-2

Because He Is
the Light of the World

*L*ord, help me to trust Your light in me and in my life. I look to You to be my treasure in darkness. Help me always remember that even when I go through the difficult and dark times in my life, You will always be there to shine Your light on my path.

The path of the just is like a shining sun, that shines ever brighter unto the perfect day.

PROVERBS 4:18

Because He Is
the Light of the World

◈◈◈

I praise You, Jesus, as the Light of the World. Your light is *in* me because *You* are *in* me, and nothing will ever change that. I know that You are light and in You is no darkness at all (1 John 1:5). Send out Your light and Your truth! Let them lead me; let them bring me to Your holy hill (Psalm 43:3). Lord, You see what is in the dark (Daniel 2:22). And when I am in darkness, You will be my light (Micah 7:8). I know that when I fall, You will lift me up again. I worship You as the Light of my life and thank You that Your light can never be put out.

◈◈

For You will light my lamp; the LORD my God will enlighten my darkness.

PSALM 18:28

Because He Is the Light of the World

Lord, You are the light of the world, and I declare You to be Lord over every nation of the earth. I know Your light will always prevail. Establish Your kingdom on earth and help us, Your children, to be a people through whom Your light shines and through whom You touch the world for Your glory. May Your light in me shine through brightly to others, so that You may be glorified.

You are the light of the world. A city that is set on a hill cannot be hidden...Let your light so shine before men, that they may see your good works and glorify your Father in heaven.

MATTHEW 5:14,16

Because He Is
the Light of the World

*L*ord, I thank You that You have called me out of the darkness to live in Your light, and to let Your light live in me. Shine Your light in any area of my life where I am not living Your way. I don't want anything that would dim Your light on my path. I don't want to give place to the darkness of this world in any way.

You are a chosen generation, a royal priesthood, a holy nation, His own special people, that you may proclaim the praises of Him who called you out of darkness into His marvelous light.

1 PETER 2:9

Because He Is

*L*ord, You are holy and righteous, and I have no greater joy in life than entering into Your presence to exalt You with worship and praise. I will bless You at all times; Your praise shall continually be in my mouth (Psalm 34:1). I welcome Your presence now. And I thank You that because You *are,* I can *be* too. I will praise You, Lord, with all my heart, and I will tell everyone of Your greatness. You make me glad, and I rejoice in You (Psalm 9:1-2). I know that in Your presence I will find everything I will ever need. I know that when I worship You, I am the closest to You I can be this side of heaven.

Blessing and honor and glory and power be to Him who sits on the throne, and to the Lamb, forever and ever!

REVELATION 5:13

Because He Is

God, I worship You. I believe that You have always been and always will be Lord over everything. My soul longs for Your courts. My heart and my flesh cry out for You, the living God (Psalm 84:1-2). I long to know You in a deeper and more intimate way. My soul hungers to be close enough to You to feel Your heartbeat and sense Your love flowing into my being. I want to know everything there is to know about You. Fill my heart with such great knowledge of You that praising You becomes like the air I breathe. I want to show my love for You by embracing You with my worship. All honor, glory, and majesty belong to You.

Whoever offers praise glorifies Me; and to him who orders his conduct aright I will show the salvation of God.

PSALM 50:23

When I Am Troubled by Negative Thoughts and Emotions

*L*ord, I praise You and thank You that You have given me a sound mind. I lay claim to that this day. Thank You that You are not the author of confusion but of peace (1 Corinthians 14:33). I choose peace this day, and I worship You, the God of peace. Thank You that I have the mind of Christ (1 Corinthians 2:16). Thank You that You enable me to cast down every argument and high thing that exalts itself against the knowledge of You and bring every thought into captivity to the obedience of Christ (2 Corinthians 10:5). Help me to be renewed in my mind and put on the new person You created me to be in righteousness and holiness (Ephesians 4:22-24).

If anyone is in Christ, he is a new creation; old things have passed away; behold, all things have become new.

2 CORINTHIANS 5:17

When I Am Troubled by Negative Thoughts and Emotions

*L*ord, I worship You. You are my Lord and King, my precious Redeemer. There is no other God like You, entirely full of goodness, grace, and mercy. You heal us when we are brokenhearted and bandage our wounds. You build us up when we are weak in our soul (Psalm 147:1-4). You are great and powerful, O Lord, and You understand all things, even what is in my heart (Psalm 147:5). Thank You that I don't have to live with sadness, hurt, or depression. This day I put on the garment of praise in exchange for the spirit of heaviness (Isaiah 61:1-3), and I glorify You as Lord of all. Thank You that You put gladness in my heart (Psalm 4:7).

You have turned for me my mourning into dancing; You have put off my sackcloth and clothed me with gladness, to the end that my glory may sing praise to You and not be silent. O LORD my God, I will give thanks to You forever.

PSALM 30:11-12

When I Have Anxiety, Fear, and Discouragement

*L*ord, I give all of my anxiety and fear to You. I surrender my hold on them and release them into Your hands. I lift my eyes to You, for You are my help in time of trouble. I will praise You in the midst of all that happens in my life. I know that in Your presence I don't need to be anxious or afraid of anything. I refuse to entertain discouragement and instead choose this day to find my encouragement in You. Your love comforts me and takes away all my fear. Your power in my life gives me strength and makes me secure. Thank You for giving me the courage to go forward and fulfill the destiny You have for me.

This poor man cried out, and the LORD heard him, and saved him out of all his troubles. The angel of the LORD encamps all around those who fear Him, and delivers them.

PSALM 34:6-7

When I Have Anxiety, Fear, and Discouragement

❦

*L*ord, I know from Your Word that I don't have to be anxious, fearful, or discouraged. I therefore release to You all feelings like that and ask You to replace them with Your peace, love, and encouragement. Enable me to identify others who may be experiencing similar feelings so that I can pray with and for them. Help me to come alongside them in prayer the way You, Holy Spirit, come alongside of me to bring me comfort.

❦

Bear one another's burdens, and so fulfill the law of Christ.

GALATIANS 6:2

When I Have Anxiety, Fear, and Discouragement

*O*Lord, I worship You above all else. You are my light and my salvation; whom shall I fear? You, Lord, are the strength of my life; of whom shall I be afraid? (Psalm 27:1). I thank You that though an army may encamp against me, my heart shall not fear (Psalm 27:3). In You, Lord, I have put my trust; I will not be afraid. What can man do to me? (Psalm 56:11). Whenever I am afraid, I will trust in You (Psalm 56:3). Thank You, Lord, that when I seek You, You hear me and deliver me from all my fears, that You save me out of all my troubles. Thank You that Your angel camps around me to deliver me (Psalm 34:4-7).

I cried to the LORD with my voice, and He heard me from His holy hill. I lay down and slept; I awoke, for the LORD sustained me. I will not be afraid of ten thousands of people who have set themselves against me all around.

PSALM 3:4-6

When I Have Anxiety, Fear, and Discouragement

*L*ord, help me to not be afraid when bad things happen, knowing You are my refuge and my strength, a very present help in trouble. Even if the world falls apart, even though the mountains are carried into the midst of the sea, I don't have to fear. Raise me up to be a powerful praying servant of Yours who lives anxious for nothing and fearful of no one. Help me to find encouragement in You and Your Word.

Give ear, O Lord, to my prayer; and attend to the voice of my supplications. In the day of my trouble I will call upon You, for You will answer me.

PSALM 86:6-7

When I Have Anxiety, Fear, and Discouragement

*L*ord, I know Your thoughts toward me are of peace, to give me a future and a hope (Jeremiah 29:11). I know that You have saved me and called me with a holy calling, not according to my works, but according to Your own purpose and grace (2 Timothy 1:9). Thank You, Holy Spirit, that You are always with me and will guide me on the path so that I won't lose my way. Give me great faith so that I am planted strong in You and not tossed about by the winds of fear, anxiety, or discouragement. I reach out for Your hand today so I can walk with You into the future You have for me.

Those who are planted in the house of the Lord shall flourish in the courts of our God. They shall still bear fruit in old age; they shall be fresh and flourishing, to declare that the Lord is upright.

PSALM 92:13-15

When I Become Sick, Weak, or Injured

*L*ord, I lift up to You my affliction this day (name it before the Lord), and I ask You to take it away. I thank You for Your grace and mercy toward me. I will extol You, O LORD, for You have lifted me up. O LORD my God, I cried out to You, and You healed me (Psalm 30:1-2). Bless the LORD, O my soul, and forget not all His benefits: who forgives all your iniquities, who heals all your diseases (Psalm 103:2-3). Should You decide not to heal me in the way and time I desire, I trust that You will bring good out of my suffering and that it will glorify You.

Heal me, O LORD, and I shall be healed; save me, and I shall be saved, for You are my praise.

JEREMIAH 17:14

When I Become Sick, Weak, or Injured

I praise You, Jesus. I exalt and thank You that You are my Healer. Thank You for dying for me on the cross, for bearing the consequences of my sin in Your body. You are greater than anything I face or suffer, and I thank You that in Your name I can find healing. Your power is unlimited. I know that if You heal me, I will be healed completely. Thank You that You will rise up with healing for those who fear Your name (Malachi 4:2). Be merciful to me, O God, be merciful to me! For my soul trusts in You; and in the shadow of Your wings I will make my refuge, until these calamities have passed by (Psalm 57:1).

He sent His word and healed them, and delivered them from their destructions.

PSALM 107:20

When I Struggle
with Doubt

*L*ord, it is by faith we stand (2 Corinthians 1:24). I want to have so much faith that I am fully convinced that whatever You have promised to me, You will also be able to perform it in my life (Romans 4:21). I know that faith is a gift from You, and I pray that my faith, no matter how it is tested by fire, will glorify You and bring all the praise and honor and glory that belong to You. Thank You that You have given me Your Word whereby my faith can be increased. Help me to grow in my understanding of it. May Your Word be so mixed with my faith that it will glorify You (Hebrews 4:2).

Now faith is the substance of things hoped for, the evidence of things not seen.

HEBREWS 11:1

When I Struggle
with Doubt

*L*ord, give me direction to know how to pray in every situation and for every concern. Make me bold to ask. Enable me to ask according to Your will. Give me faith to believe that impossible things can happen when I pray. Forgive me when I have any doubt about Your ability to answer. I confess all doubt in me as sin and ask You to cleanse me of it. Replace doubt with strong faith that all things are possible because I trust in You.

If you can believe, all things are possible to him who believes.

MARK 9:23

When I Struggle with Doubt

I worship You, Almighty God, and give You all the glory that is due Your name. I praise You, Lord of heaven and earth, and thank You that with You all things are possible. The things that are impossible with men are possible with You (Luke 18:27). Thank You that You give faith as a gift to those who ask. Because of You, I don't have to live in doubt. I ask You to increase my faith to believe for bigger and greater things. Help me to always ask in faith, with no doubting. May I never be like a wave of the sea driven and tossed by the wind because I have doubt (James 1:6-8).

In this you greatly rejoice, though now for a little while, if need be, you have been grieved by various trials, that the genuineness of your faith, being much more precious than gold that perishes, though it is tested by fire, may be found to praise, honor, and glory at the revelation of Jesus Christ.

1 PETER 1:6-7

When I Don't See Answers to My Prayers

❧

Lord, I know that what I may see as unanswered prayer may not be unanswered at all. It means that You are answering according to Your will. Whether I understand Your will or not doesn't affect the fact that I trust it and praise You for it. Thank You for Your unfailing Word and that You always keep Your promises to me. I thank You that Your power is infinite. Your judgments and Your will are perfect, and I trust them. Whether or not my prayers are answered the way I pray them, I will praise and worship You above all things. For You are my Wonderful Counselor, my Everlasting Father, my Stronghold in the Day of Trouble, and my Resting Place. I rest in You today.

❧

Do not throw away your confidence; it will be richly rewarded. You need to persevere so that when you have done the will of God, you will receive what he has promised.

HEBREWS 10:35-36 NIV

When I Don't See Answers to My Prayers

*L*ord, I thank You for the privilege of speaking to You in prayer. Increase my faith to believe that I can make a difference when I pray. And when I don't see answers to my prayers exactly the way I prayed them, help me to not allow myself to get discouraged and lose faith. Help me trust You to answer in Your way and Your timing.

Men always ought to pray and not lose heart.

LUKE 18:1

When I Don't See Answers to My Prayers

Lord, I worship You as the all-knowing and all-powerful God of the universe. You are Immanuel, God with us. Thank You that You are always with me. Thank You that Your presence frees me from all doubt and gives me increased faith. Thank You that You hear my prayers and will answer in Your time and in Your way. You, Lord, are without limitations. I don't want to limit Your working in my life by my own faithlessness. Help me to be joyful in hope, patient in affliction, faithful in prayer (Romans 12:12 NIV). I know that You have called me to pray, but I also know that answering prayers is Your job. Help my heart to rest in You.

Continue earnestly in prayer, being vigilant in it with thanksgiving.

COLOSSIANS 4:2

When I Have Problems
in a Relationship

*L*ord, I praise You as the God of restoration, for I know You can restore my relationships to complete wholeness. Help me to be in unity with others and to be compassionate, loving, tenderhearted, and courteous, not returning evil for evil, but rather only giving blessings to them (1 Peter 3:8-9). I praise You as my Creator and recognize that You created all the people with whom I am in relationship. You are their heavenly Father just as You are mine. They are my brothers and sisters, and You love and forgive them as You love and forgive me. You laid down Your life for them as You laid it down for me. Help me to love them as You love me.

Since you have purified your souls in obeying the truth through the Spirit in sincere love of the brethren, love one another fervently with a pure heart.

1 PETER 1:22

When I Have Problems in a Relationship

*L*ord, I worship You. I praise You, precious God of love, and thank You that You have poured out Your love on me. I lift my heart to You and ask You to fill it so full of Your unfailing and unconditional love that it overflows onto others. Thank You, Lord, that You are the God who makes all things new, even our relationships. You can put new love in our heart. You can revive love that has died and make love live again. I give all of my relationships to You and thank You for them. For those who are closest and most important to me, and those who are most challenging and difficult, enable me to love them the way You do.

A new commandment I give to you, that you love one another; as I have loved you, that you also love one another.

JOHN 13:34

When I Need to Forgive

*I*t amazes me, Lord, that You love me so much that You would sacrifice Yourself so I could be forgiven completely. Your unfailing love is better to me than life itself. Thank You that You love me, even though You have seen me at my worst. Help me to be that same way toward others. Thank You, heavenly Father, that You are rich in mercy and grace toward me, and Your love and mercy are everlasting. Help me to become the loving and forgiving person You want me to be.

Be kind to one another, tenderhearted, forgiving one another, just as God in Christ forgave you.

EPHESIANS 4:32

When I Need
to Forgive

*L*ord, I worship You for who You are. I praise You, my precious and loving God of forgiveness. Thank You for forgiving me. Where would I be without You setting me free from the consequences of my own sin? Lord, I surrender to You everything that is in my heart. I want to be a forgiving person so I will always be forgiven (Matthew 6:14-15). Take away anything in me that separates me from You and hinders my knowing You better. Pour out Your Spirit upon me in a fresh new way and reveal anyone or anything that I have not forgiven. Shine Your light into the corners of my heart and reveal anything that is not of You.

The discretion of a man makes him slow to anger, and his glory is to overlook a transgression.

PROVERBS 19:11

When I See Things Going Wrong and Feel Powerless

*L*ord, whenever I go through tough times, when everything seems to be going wrong, help me to draw near to You and disengage from the concerns of this life. I thank You that You are able to do exceedingly abundantly above all that I ask or think, according to Your power that works in me (Ephesians 3:20). I worship You, God of grace, and thank You that after I have suffered a while, You will perfect, establish, strengthen, and settle me (1 Peter 5:10-11). I praise and thank You for Your power and that You will infuse Your power into me in great measure. I worship You, Father of mercy and comfort, and thank You that You comfort me in my times of trial.

My brethren, count it all joy when you fall into various trials, knowing that the testing of your faith produces patience. But let patience have its perfect work, that you may be perfect and complete, lacking nothing.

JAMES 1:2-4

When I See Things Going Wrong and Feel Powerless

*L*ord, help me to remember that when it seems to me as though things are going wrong, they may not be wrong at all. It may be that You are allowing these things to happen in order to bring me to a place of total dependence upon You so that Your purposes can be accomplished in my life. I trust that You have a purpose for every storm in my life, and when I pray and trust You, You will deliver me out of it.

The effective, fervent prayer of a righteous man avails much.

JAMES 5:16

When I See Things Going Wrong and Feel Powerless

*L*ord, I praise Your name. I exalt You above all things. You are my King and Lord. In the midst of everything that is happening in my life and all that I am going through, I know that You are the all-powerful God of the universe. Hide me in Your secret place in my time of struggle. Lift me high upon a rock so that I may rise above the plans of my enemies to surround me with problems. I will sing and offer You the sacrifice of praise (Psalm 27:5-6). You are my help, and I will hide myself in You. I praise You for all that You are. My soul follows close behind You; Your right hand upholds me (Psalm 63:8).

Beloved, do not think it strange concerning the fiery trial which is to try you, as though some strange thing happened to you; but rejoice to the extent that you partake of Christ's sufferings, that when His glory is revealed, you may also be glad with exceeding joy.

1 PETER 4:12-13

When I Long to Know God's Will

*L*ord, I worship You and praise You as the all-knowing and all-wise God of the universe. All things are known by You. You know all of my days, and You know the way I should go. Thank You that You give wisdom to those who ask for it. And I ask for wisdom today. I know that having mere knowledge apart from You will never be enough to satisfy the longing in my heart. I can never know enough. What I need to know, only You can teach me. Lord, I know it is Your will for me to give thanks *in* all things, so I thank You this day *for* everything You have done in my life (1 Thessalonians 5:18).

For this reason we also, since the day we heard it, do not cease to pray for you, and to ask that you may be filled with the knowledge of His will in all wisdom and spiritual understanding; that you may walk worthy of the Lord, fully pleasing Him, being fruitful in every good work and increasing in the knowledge of God.

COLOSSIANS 1:9-10

When I Long to Know God's Will

*H*eavenly Father, help me to live in Your will. Thank You that Your will is not beyond knowing and that You reveal Yourself to me when I ask You to. Help me to abide in You so that I can understand Your ways and Your heart. With every decision I must make, I ask that You would give me wisdom, revelation, and clear leading from Your Holy Spirit.

By this we know that we abide in Him, and He in us, because He has given us of His Spirit.

1 JOHN 4:13

When I Long to Know God's Will

*L*ord, thank You for giving me knowledge of Your will in all wisdom and spiritual understanding (Colossians 1:9). Thank You for guiding me and leading me. Thank You for giving me understanding from Your Word and directing my steps so I can stay on the path You have for me. Thank You for revealing to me the way in which I should go regarding every decision I make. I praise You for Your wisdom and knowledge and revelation. Thank You for helping me to stand perfect and complete in the center of Your will (Colossians 4:12). Give me the endurance I need, so that after I have done Your will, I will receive the promise (Hebrews 10:36).

He who does the will of God abides forever.

1 JOHN 2:17

When I Seek Breakthrough, Deliverance, or Transformation

Heavenly Father, thank You that You have delivered me out of the enemy's hand. I know You will continue to deliver me until the day I go to be with You. I call upon Your name, Lord. I implore You, deliver my soul (Psalm 116:4). I know You have begun a good work in me and You will complete it (Philippians 1:6). I know that in whatever state I am, I can be content because You will not leave me there forever (Philippians 4:11). I will praise You in the midst of any need I have for breakthrough, deliverance, or transformation, knowing that You see my need and will meet it in Your way and in Your time.

Do not remember the former things, nor consider the things of old. Behold, I will do a new thing, now it shall spring forth; shall you not know it? I will even make a road in the wilderness and rivers in the desert.

ISAIAH 43:18-19

When I Seek Breakthrough, Deliverance, or Transformation

*L*ord, I know that wherever I am locked up in my life, You can set me free. I ask You to do that today. I invite Your presence in a new and powerful way right now to bring deliverance and transformation. I know that where Your Spirit is, there is liberty (2 Corinthians 3:17).

We had the sentence of death in ourselves, that we should not trust in ourselves, but in God who raises the dead, who delivered us from so great a death and does deliver us; in whom we trust that He will still deliver us.

2 CORINTHIANS 1:9-10

When I Seek Breakthrough, Deliverance, or Transformation

I worship You, Lord. You are my rock, my fortress, my deliverer, my strength in whom I trust, my shield, my stronghold, and my salvation (Psalm 18:2). You looked down from above and drew me out of many waters (Psalm 18:16). You have brought me into a broad place and You have delivered me because You delighted in me (Psalm 18:19). You are my God and I will praise You (Exodus 15:2). Lord, I praise You as my Almighty Deliverer. You have the power to set me free and transform my life. Thank You that You will break down every stronghold that the enemy of my soul has erected in and around me. You will break down every wall that separates me from all You have for me.

The Lord will deliver me from every evil work and preserve me for His heavenly kingdom. To Him be glory forever and ever.

2 TIMOTHY 4:18

When I Need God's Provision and Protection

❧❧❧

I love You, Lord. I know that Your provision and protection are evidence of Your great love for me. I call upon You, for You are worthy to be praised, and You will save me from my enemies (Psalm 18:3). I rejoice in You, I trust in You, I shout for joy because You defend me. Thank You that You bless and surround me like a shield (Psalm 5:11-12). You are my God, and I am one of Your sheep for whom You extend Your hand of protection (Psalm 95:6-7). You are my refuge and my strength in the day of trouble, and I will sing Your praises forever (Psalm 59:16-17).

❧❧

The LORD is my strength and my shield; my heart trusted in Him, and I am helped; therefore my heart greatly rejoices, and with my song I will praise Him.

PSALM 28:7

When I Need God's Provision and Protection

*L*ord, You are King and Lord over all my life. I surrender everything I have to You because I recognize that every good thing I have has been given to me by You as a sign of Your goodness, mercy, and love (James 1:17). Thank You that You are my Provider and You provide everything I need. Lord, I praise You as my Protector. Thank You for hiding me under the shadow of Your wings, from the wicked who oppress me, from my deadly enemies who surround me (Psalm 17:8-9). I give praise to You, for You have delivered my soul from death. You have kept my feet from falling, so that I may walk before You in the light of the living? (Psalm 56:12-13).

*Those who seek the L*ORD *shall not lack any good thing.*

PSALM 34:10

When I Fight Temptation to Walk in the Flesh

*L*ord, when I am tempted, show me what it is that is drawing me away from You. I praise You in the midst of any temptation I am facing, knowing You have the power to break its hold on me. Help me to walk in the Spirit so that I will not fulfill the lust of the flesh (Galatians 5:16). Lord, I know that it is no longer I who live, but Christ who lives in me; and the life which I now live in the flesh I live by faith (Galatians 2:20). Thank You that You give me strength to resist anything that would entice me away from a close walk with You.

For we do not have a High Priest who cannot sympathize with our weaknesses, but was in all points tempted as we are, yet without sin.

HEBREWS 4:15

When I Fight Temptation to Walk in the Flesh

*L*ord, I thank You that You are able to lift me out of the realm of the flesh and into the realm of the Spirit, out of a condition of emptiness and into one of fulfillment, out of what is worthless and into what is worthwhile. I reach up to You right now and ask You to set me free from anything that tempts me to walk in the flesh and not in the Spirit.

So then, those who are in the flesh cannot please God. But you are not in the flesh but in the Spirit, if indeed the Spirit of God dwells in you.

ROMANS 8:8-9

When I Fight Temptation
to Walk in the Flesh

*L*ord, I worship You as my Lord and Savior. I praise You, Holy Spirit, that You live in me and enable me to move in the Spirit and not the flesh. I confess all my sins before You and repent of them. Specifically I confess (tell God anything you feel you need to confess). I don't want any sin in my life. God, help me to trust Your ways and love Your laws enough to always obey them. Help me to have such faith in Your goodness that obeying Your commands and directives is never even a question for me. Enable me to live in obedience. Make me walk in the path of Your commandments, for I delight in it (Psalm 119:35).

No temptation has overtaken you except such as is common to man; but God is faithful, who will not allow you to be tempted beyond what you are able, but with the temptation will also make the way of escape, that you may be able to bear it.

1 CORINTHIANS 10:13

When I Am Attacked by the Enemy

⁕

Lord, I praise You as my Deliverer and thank You that You will deliver me from my enemies. I know that we do not wrestle against flesh and blood, but against principalities, against powers, against the rulers of the darkness of this age, against spiritual hosts of wickedness in the heavenly places (Ephesians 6:12). You will lift me up above those who rise against me and deliver me from the violent forces that oppose me. Lead me, O LORD, in Your righteousness because of my enemies; make Your way straight before my face (Psalm 5:8). I give thanks to You, Lord, and sing praises to Your name (Psalm 18:49). Thank You that You always lead us in triumph in Christ (2 Corinthians 2:14).

⁕

No weapon formed against you shall prosper, and every tongue which rises against you in judgment you shall condemn. This is the heritage of the servants of the LORD, and their righteousness is from Me, says the LORD.

ISAIAH 54:17

When I Am
Attacked by the Enemy

*L*ord, I thank You that You have already defeated the enemy. I submit to You this day and resist the onslaught of the enemy upon my life, knowing that he will flee from me (James 4:7). I worship You in the midst of everything I face, knowing that in Your presence there is safety and peace.

> *He delivered me from my strong enemy, from those who hated me, for they were too strong for me...He delivered me because He delighted in me.*

PSALM 18:17,19

When I Am Attacked by the Enemy

Lord, I worship You as Lord over everything. I praise You as my all-powerful King. You, Lord, You are a shield to all who trust in You (Psalm 18:28-30). I will not be afraid nor dismayed because of the force of evil that comes against me, for I know that the battle is not mine but Yours. I know that I will not need to fight this battle alone. Instead, I will position myself in a stance of praise and worship toward You, and I will stand still and see Your salvation, for You are with me (2 Chronicles 20:15-17). Thank You that You will deliver me from the enemy and enable me to stand strong.

Be strong in the Lord and in the power of His might. Put on the whole armor of God, that you may be able to stand against the wiles of the devil.

EPHESIANS 6:10-11

When I Suffer Great Loss, Disappointment, or Failure

❧❧❧

I praise You and worship You, Lord. I love You and recognize that all I have is from You. Everything I have is Yours, and I surrender it all to You for Your glory. Therefore, whatever I have lost I release into Your hands. I praise You and thank You that this is the day that You have made, and I will rejoice and be glad in it. Thank You for Your grace and mercy. Thank You that You love me the way You do. Thank You that You will bring good out of my situation. No matter what has happened or will happen in my life, as long as I am alive I will sing praises to You (Psalm 146:1-2).

❧

These things I have spoken to you, that in Me you may have peace. In the world you will have tribulation; but be of good cheer, I have overcome the world.

JOHN 16:33

When I Suffer Great Loss, Disappointment, or Failure

O God, You are Lord over heaven and on earth and Lord over my life. I praise You, my precious Redeemer and King. I thank You that You are a God of redemption and restoration. I surrender to You all my grief or sadness over any loss, disappointment, or failure I have experienced and praise You in the midst of it. I thank You, Holy Spirit, that You are my Comforter. Lord, I thank You that You allow no suffering that is without purpose. I know that You are a good God and what You allow will be used for good. I draw close to You and put my hope in You, for with You there is mercy and redemption (Psalm 130:7).

You number my wanderings; put my tears into Your bottle; are they not in Your book? When I cry out to You, then my enemies will turn back; this I know, because God is for me.

PSALM 56:8-9

When I Sense
that All Is Well

*L*ord, I worship You for all that You are. You are Lord over the good times as well as the difficult. Lord on the mountaintop as well as the valley. You are King of kings on the throne of my life in the calm as well as in the storm. I want to show my love for You every day by embracing You with my worship and touching You with my praise. Fill my heart with such great knowledge of You that praising You becomes a way of life. Teach me to make praise my first reaction to every situation, no matter what the situation is. I have no greater joy in life than entering into Your presence to exalt You with worship and praise every day.

As you have therefore received Christ Jesus the Lord, so walk in Him, rooted and built up in Him and established in the faith, as you have been taught, abounding in it with thanksgiving.

COLOSSIANS 2:6-7

When I Sense
that All Is Well

$\mathcal{L}$ord, I thank You for the times when things are going well. During those times, help me to not take Your goodness for granted. I know it is good to give thanks to You no matter what is happening (Psalm 92:1) for this is Your will (1 Thessalonians 5:18). In all things—good and bad—You are deserving of praise. Remind me of all the things You have taught me so that I will continue to do them diligently.

You must continue in the things you have learned and been assured of, knowing from whom you have learned them.

1 TIMOTHY 3:14

When I Sense
that All Is Well

*L*ord, I worship You for all that You are. You are my Lord in the good times as well as the difficult. On the mountaintop as well as in the valley. I praise You in times of great blessing as well as in times of great challenge. It is because of You that I can stand strong, even when I feel weak. For I know that when I am weakest, You show Yourself strong. I am grateful for Your salvation, deliverance, protection, goodness, and blessings in my life every day. I know that everything I have comes from You. Because of Your great strength I go from glory to glory and strength to strength no matter what is happening in my life (Psalm 84:7).

Let him who thinks he stands take heed lest he fall.

1 CORINTHIANS 10:12

PART III

Just Enough Light
for the
STEP I'M ON

Learning to Walk

*L*ord, I don't want to take one step without You. I reach up for Your hand and ask that You lead me in Your way. Thank You that no matter where I am right now, even if I have gotten way off course, in this moment as I put my hand in Yours, You will make a path from where I am to where I need to be. And You will lead me on it. Thank You that Your grace abounds to me in that way. Keep me on the path You have for me and take me where You want me to go. I commit this day to walking with You.

You will show me the path of life; in Your presence is fullness of joy; at Your right hand are pleasures forevermore.

PSALM 16:11

Learning to Walk

*L*ord, I thank You that You are teaching me how to walk with You. If the path I am on is crooked, I pray You will make it straight. If I am going in the wrong direction, I pray you will turn me around and set me on the correct path. I know that as I take one step at a time, holding on to You and letting You lead, You will get me where I need to go.

O Lord, I know the way of man is not in himself;
it is not in man who walks to direct his own steps.

JEREMIAH 10:23

Learning to Walk

*L*ord, "cause me to know the way in which I should walk, for I lift up my soul to You" (Psalm 143:8). I know that when I try to run the race without You, I get off course. Thank You that even if I become weak and stumble, You will help me to rise again and continue on. And though I can't see exactly where I am going, I'm certain that You can and will enable me to get to where I need to be. Thank You, Lord, that You are teaching me how to walk in total dependence upon You, for I know therein lies my greatest blessing.

Come, and let us go up to the mountain of the Lord, to the house of the God of Jacob; He will teach us His ways, and we shall walk in His paths.

MICAH 4:2

Learning to Walk

*L*ord, I am committed to walking with You. Show me any place in my life where I have not taken the steps You want me to take. Help me to hear Your voice guiding me where I need to go. I surrender my life to You completely so that You can lead me on the path You have for me. I want to become more and more dependent upon You every day of my life. Help me to do that. I trust that Your ways are best, and I know that You always have my best interests in mind.

The steps of a good man are ordered by the Lord, and He delights in his way.

PSALM 37:23

Beginning to See the Light

*L*ord, I trust You with all my heart, and I will not lean on my own understanding. I acknowledge You in all my ways and ask You to direct my paths. Order my day and be in charge of it. Help me to do all I need to do.

A man's heart plans his way, but the LORD directs his steps.

PROVERBS 16:9

Beginning to See the Light

*L*ord, You are the light of my life. You illuminate my path, and I will follow wherever You lead. Protect me from being blinded by the light that confuses. Help me to always identify the counterfeit. I depend on You to lift up the light of Your countenance upon me (Psalm 4:6). Thank You, Lord, that because You never change, Your light is constant in my life no matter what is going on around me. Shine Your light through me as I walk with my hand in Yours. I give this day to You and trust that the light You give me is just the amount I need for the step I'm on.

The path of the just is like the shining sun, that shines ever brighter unto the perfect day.

PROVERBS 4:18

Beginning to See the Light

*L*ord, I pray that I will not be deceived and drawn toward the glittering light of the enemy. Help me to discern his deceptive tactics. Forgive me for the times I felt I was in the dark because I didn't recognize Your light in me. Help me to grow in faith so that I always trust You, the light of the world, to lead me through any dark times that come. May I never look to anything or anyone outside of You, Jesus, as a source of guiding light for my life.

This is the message which we have heard from Him and declare to you, that God is light and in Him is no darkness at all. If we say that we have fellowship with Him, and walk in darkness, we lie and do not practice the truth. But if we walk in the light as He is in the light, we have fellowship with one another, and the blood of Jesus Christ His Son cleanses us from all sin.

1 JOHN 1:5-7

Beginning to See the Light

*L*ord, I confess as sin any time in my life when I was going through a dark or difficult situation and I doubted You were there for me. Forgive me for that misunderstanding. I know now that You will never leave me nor forsake me. Help me to always trust Your Spirit in me to illuminate the path ahead as I walk on it with You. I acknowledge that You are the true Light who gives light to the world (John 1:9). Thank You that Your light will never be put out, and I can never really be in darkness when I look to You.

"While you have the light, believe in the light, that you may become sons of light." These things Jesus spoke, and departed, and was hidden from them.

JOHN 12:36

Beginning to See the Light

*L*ord, I realize I am powerless to do anything of significance or accomplish anything lasting without You. I know it is not by my strength or wisdom that powerful things happen in my life, but it is by Your Spirit. My prayers are not answered because of *what* I know, but because of *whom* I know. Thank You that I have come to know You as the light of my world. Thank You for the light of Your Spirit that I experience every day. Help me to truly see Your light more and more, and to trust that it is always there because You are always there.

In Him was life, and the life was the light of men.

JOHN 1:4

Refusing to Be Afraid
of the Dark

*L*ord, thank You that because I walk with You I don't have to fear the dark. Even in the blackest night, You are there. In the darkest times, You have treasures for me. No matter what I am going through, Your presence and grace are my comfort and my light. Your Word says, "if one walks in the night, he stumbles, because the light is not in him" (John 11:9-10). But I know Your light *is* in me. Jesus, You have come as a light into the world so that whoever believes in You should not abide in darkness (John 12:46).

Even the night shall be light about me; indeed, the darkness shall not hide from You, but the night shines as the day; the darkness and the light are both alike to You.

PSALM 139:11-12

Refusing to Be Afraid of the Dark

*L*ord, I believe in You and know that You have lifted me out of the darkness of hopelessness, futility, and fear. I refuse to be afraid. I confess any time I have chosen to walk in the darkness of doubt, disobedience, or blaming You for my circumstances. Forgive me. I give my hand to You, Lord. Take hold of it and lead me. Thank You that as I take each step, the light You give me will be all I need.

Who walks in darkness and has no light? Let him trust in the name of the LORD and rely upon his God.

ISAIAH 50:10

Refusing to Be Afraid
of the Dark

*L*ord, lift the blinders off of me so that I can see the truth about myself and my situation. If I find myself in a dark circumstance because of my own disobedience, help me to understand that so I can confess it and get back on the path. But if it is a darkness that You are allowing, help me to reach out to you in total dependence and find Your light in it. I know that the treasure I find in darkness is You.

I will give you the treasures of darkness and hidden riches of secret places, that you may know that I, the LORD, who call you by your name, am the God of Israel.

ISAIAH 45:3

Refusing to Be Afraid
of the Dark

*L*ord, I regard Your presence and my relationship with You as the most important thing in my life. Help me to never doubt it or take it for granted. In the times when You are testing my faith and my love for You, I pray that I will draw ever closer to You. Even in the most difficult situation of my life right now, I know that You are in control and will turn things around and bring good out of it. I refuse to allow fear or a lack of faith to keep me from walking victoriously in all You have for me.

For You will light my lamp; the LORD my God will enlighten my darkness.

PSALM 18:28

Embracing the Moment

*L*ord, You are everything to me. Thank You that I can walk each moment with You and not have to figure life out on my own. And when I come to a dark time, I can put my hand in Yours and depend on You as we walk through it together. I know that "the upright shall dwell in Your presence" (Psalm 140:13), and that's where I want to live. For in Your presence I will find healing, deliverance, love, peace, joy, and hope.

For our light affliction, which is but for a moment, is working for us a far more exceeding and eternal weight of glory, while we do not look at the things which are seen, but at the things which are not seen. For the things which are seen are temporary, but the things which are not seen are eternal.

2 CORINTHIANS 4:17-18

Embracing the Moment

*L*ord, help me to embrace the moments of my life that are hard to get my arms around. Enable my eyes to see You in them. Help me to always acknowledge the abundance of Your goodness to me. I lift to You the deepest struggles in my life. I trust You to open my eyes to see all You have for me in them. Reveal to me the fullness of it all. Thank You that I can be filled with the joy of Your presence in every step I take, because You have given me the light I need for whatever step I am on.

In the day when I cried out, You answered me, and made me bold with strength in my soul.

PSALM 138:3

Embracing the Moment

*L*ord, help me to be content where I am right now on Your path for my life. I know You are always growing me into Your likeness and will not leave me where I am forever. I resolve to see any loneliness or lack of contentment in me as a sign that I need to spend more time with You. Help me to recognize Your blessings and goodness in the midst of every situation I face. Give me strength when I am weary and the fullness of Your joy when I feel sad. Help me to have an ever-increasing faith and a greater sense of Your presence in my life.

Though I walk in the midst of trouble, You will revive me; You will stretch out Your hand against the wrath of my enemies, and Your right hand will save me.

PSALM 138:7

Embracing the Moment

*L*ord, I know that regardless of what situation I am in right now, You have an abundance of blessings for me. Right where I am, You are working powerfully in my life. Thank You for saving me, Jesus, and setting me free from all that would keep me from moving into everything You have for me. Thank You for filling me with Your Holy Spirit. Thank You for loving me.

The love of God has been poured out in our hearts by the Holy Spirit who was given to us.

ROMANS 5:5

Dancing in the Footlights

*L*ord, shine the light of Your Word on the path of my life today. Make it a lamp for my feet so that I do not stumble. Bring it alive in my spirit so that it illuminates my mind and soul. Let it be a guide for every decision I make, every step I take. Keep me from turning to the right or the left so that I will stay on the narrow path that leads to life. Help me daily to carve out time to be alone with You and to feed on Your truth.

Great peace have those who love Your law, and nothing causes them to stumble.

PSALM 119:165

Dancing in the Footlights

Lord, "oh, how I love Your law! It is my meditation all the day" (Psalm 119:97). Open my eyes to see new treasure every time I read or hear it. Speak to me and comfort my heart. Make Your Word come alive in me and use it to nourish my soul and spirit like food does for my body. Align my heart with Yours and give me revelation and guidance so that I may know Your will for my life. Shine the light of truth where I am right now and show me the next step to take.

The entrance of Your words gives light; it gives understanding to the simple.

PSALM 119:130

Dancing in the Footlights

*L*ord, just as the footlights on the stage show a performer where to step so as not to fall, so does Your Word light the path I'm on so that I will not stumble. I pray that the light I receive from Your Word will be renewed and reestablished every day, so that my feet are always on solid ground.

Oh, send out Your light and Your truth! Let them lead me; let them bring me to Your holy hill.

PSALM 43:3

Dancing in the Footlights

*L*ord, help me to spend more time in Your Word. Open my eyes to really see Your truth as I read it. Engrave it upon my soul so that it makes changes in me that last. As I read it, may it give me clarity, peace, security, and direction. Help me to remember to use Your Word as a weapon against the enemy of my soul. Fortify me with Your double-edged sword that is more powerful than any weapon the enemy would try to use against me. May Your Word bring light to any dark areas of my life. May it set my soul free so my heart may dance for joy in Your presence.

For the word of God is living and powerful, and sharper than any two-edged sword, piercing even to the division of soul and spirit, and of joints and marrow, and is a discerner of the thoughts and intents of the heart.

HEBREWS 4:12

Praying Your Light Bill

❦

*L*ord, I thank You that You have given me all the light I need for this day. I want to experience everything You have for me, and I am willing to pay the price of obedience for it. So if there is any area in my life where I am not walking in full obedience to Your ways, show me. If You want me to do something that I am not doing, make me understand and enable me to accomplish it. Don't let me drift away. Pull me out of the darkness of deep waters and rescue me from all that takes me from You. I lay down my will and surrender to Yours.

❧

Unto the upright there arises light in the darkness; He is gracious, and full of compassion, and righteous.

PSALM 112:4

Praying Your Light Bill

*L*ord, I want to be a person who moves in Your power and whose prayers have the power to effect significant change in the world around me. Help me to always remember to live by the power of Your Spirit and not try to do things in my own strength. Show me how to use the keys You have given me to unlock and unleash Your power in prayer. Help me to pay the price for having the fullness of Your light, which is living Your way. I don't want to find myself walking in the dark because I wasn't willing to pay the price for having the light.

He shall bring forth your righteousness as the light, and your justice as the noonday.

PSALM 37:6

Praying Your Light Bill

❧

*L*ord, I know that obedience to Your ways is something You require of people who have Your light in them. Help me to turn away from any selfish claims to my own life in order to heed Your direction. Take any rebellion in me and expose it with Your truth. "Search me, O God, and know my heart; try me, and know my anxieties; and see if there is any wicked way in me, and lead me in the way everlasting" (Psalm 139:23-24). Lord, I choose this day to obey You because I know my life works best when I do. In the areas where obedience is hard for me, walk me through step by step. I don't want to do anything that would dim the light You have for my path.

❧

For everyone practicing evil hates the light and does not come to the light, lest his deeds should be exposed. But he who does the truth comes to the light, that his deeds may be clearly seen, that they have been done in God.

JOHN 3:20-21

Praying Your Light Bill

*L*ord, I thank You that You paid the price for my salvation. Help me now to pay the price of obedience for the fullness of Your light and Your presence in my life. Reveal any area of disobedience in me. Keep me aware of the subtle influences that can pull me away from the narrow path. Show me the things in my life that compete with You for my attention and attempt to get me off course. Enable me to clearly know the way You are leading me so that I am always in the right place at the right time.

Enter by the narrow gate; for wide is the gate and broad is the way that leads to destruction, and there are many who go in by it. Because narrow is the gate and difficult is the way which leads to life, and there are few who find it.

MATTHEW 7:13-14

Standing in the Line of Fire

*L*ord, I thank You for being my defender. You are more powerful than any plan the enemy has against me. Thank You that You will never leave or forsake me, and that You are always strong in my behalf. "I will lift up my eyes to the hills—from whence comes my help? My help comes from the LORD, who made heaven and earth" (Psalm 121:1-2). No matter what happens, I will look to You to deliver me from the hand of all who oppose me.

Keep me as the apple of Your eye; hide me under the shadow of Your wings, from the wicked who oppresses me, from my deadly enemies who surround me.

PSALM 17:8-9

Standing in the Line of Fire

*L*ord, I know that because I put my trust in You, You will be my shield (Proverbs 30:5). And I will not fear what man can do to me. "Lead me, O LORD, in Your righteousness because of my enemies; make Your way straight before my face" (Psalm 5:8). In myself I don't have what it takes to establish a formidable defense. I cannot protect myself and all I care about from the weapons of the enemy. But the enemy's strength is nothing to You.

Do not rejoice over me, my enemy; when I fall, I will arise; when I sit in darkness, the LORD will be a light to me.

MICAH 7:8

Standing in the Line of Fire

*L*ord, thank You that You are my defender. Help me to remember that at the first sign of enemy attack. Thank You that when the swirling waters of spiritual warfare threaten to overtake me, I can cry out to You and You will lift me up and bring me through on dry ground. It is You, O Lord, who gives strength and power to Your people (Psalm 68:35). Thank You that Your power is mighty in me.

God has power to help and to overthrow.

2 CHRONICLES 25:8

Standing in the Line of Fire

*L*ord, thank You that Your Word says that no weapon formed against me shall prosper (Isaiah 54:17). I know You have armed me with strength for the battle and will keep me safe (Psalm 18:39). Help me to "cast off the works of darkness, and put on the armor of light" (Romans 13:12). Cause a song of deliverance to rise in my heart, and I will sing praise to Your glory as You fight the battle for me. I will walk with You through the enemy's attack, knowing that Your light on my path signals my certain victory.

Be strong in the Lord and in the power of His might. Put on the whole armor of God, that you may be able to stand against the wiles of the devil.

EPHESIANS 6:10-11

See What's Right with This Picture

❧❧❧❧

*L*ord, I lay my worries before You and ask for Your mighty intervention to show me what's right when I can only see what's wrong. I am determined to see the good, so help me not to be blinded by my own fears, doubts, wants, and preconceived ideas. I ask You to reveal to me Your truth in every situation. Bless me with the ability to understand the bigger picture and to distinguish the valuable from the unimportant. When something seems to go wrong, help me not to jump to negative conclusions. Enable me to recognize the answers to my own prayers. I trust You to help me see the light in every situation.

❧❧

And we know that all things work together for good to those who love God, to those who are the called according to His purpose.

ROMANS 8:28

See What's Right
with This Picture

*L*ord, so often I have prayed for something and didn't even recognize the answer to my own prayer when I received it, because it did not happen the way I thought it would. Forgive me when I have been ungrateful because of my lack of perception. Help me to see things from Your perspective. Help me to see Your goodness in all things.

*This is the day the L*ord *has made; we will rejoice and be glad in it.*

PSALM 118:24

See What's Right
with This Picture

*L*ord, when I find myself in difficult or uncomfortable situations, show me Your perspective. Help me to see what's right and not all that appears to be wrong. Where I have failed to recognize Your hand of goodness and blessing in my circumstances, forgive me. Help me to make praise to You my first reaction to every event in my life. Deliver me from an ungrateful heart and help me not to complain when I should be giving thanks. I know You are a good God, and I trust You completely with my life. I rejoice in this day and every day because You are in charge of them all.

I would have lost heart, unless I had believed that
I would see the goodness of the LORD in the land
of the living.

PSALM 27:13

Testing, One, Two, Three

*L*ord, grow me up in Your ways and lead me in Your will. Help me to become so strong in You that I will not waver or doubt. Make me to understand Your Word and Your directions to me. "Test me, O LORD, and try me, examine my heart and my mind; for your love is ever before me, and I walk continually in your truth" (Psalm 26:2-3 NIV). I want to pass successfully through any time of testing You bring me to so that I might be refined.

You have tested my heart; You have visited me in the night; You have tried me and have found nothing; I have purposed that my mouth shall not transgress.

PSALM 17:3

Testing, One,
Two, Three

*L*ord, I don't want to wander around in the wilderness of life, going over and over the same territory because I haven't learned the lesson. I pray that I will always have a teachable heart that recognizes Your hand in my life and soaks up Your instruction. Help me to trust Your timing. Establish in me an unwavering faith so I will know that when I walk with You, even the refining fire provides the perfect light for the step I'm on.

Praise our God, O peoples, let the sound of his praise be heard; he has preserved our lives and kept our feet from slipping. For you, O God, tested us; you refined us like silver.

PSALM 66:8-10 NIV

Testing, One, Two, Three

*L*ord, I know that we are often put to our most difficult test just before the greatest work of God in our lives is about to be accomplished. Help me to remember that when I am going through a time of testing and trial. May my attitude in the midst of such times always be one of praise and worship and great faith and trust in You. Guide me through it and help me to hear You when You speak to my heart.

When He, the Spirit of truth, has come, He will guide you into all truth.

JOHN 16:13

Testing, One,
Two, Three

❦

*L*ord, help me to count it all joy when I go through trials, because I know that when You test my faith it produces good things in me. I want to have the confidence and assurance that because of You, and all You have done and are doing in my life, I am complete and not lacking anything. Help me not to fail the tests of my obedience, faith, and love for You. I want to be perfected in those areas because I know it will be for my greatest blessings. I praise You in the midst of all that is happening in my life.

❦

My brethren, count it all joy when you fall into various trials, knowing that the testing of your faith produces patience. But let patience have its perfect work, that you may be perfect and complete, lacking nothing.

JAMES 1:2-4

Knowing How to Pack
for the Wilderness

❧

*L*ord, I am at home wherever You are. Shine Your light on the path You have for me to travel, for I know all my days are in Your hands. Forgive me when I grumble or have less than a grateful heart about where I am right now. I realize my attitude will have a direct bearing on whether I wander around in circles or whether I get through to the Promised Land You have for me. Help me to trust You for every step. Enable me to see all the blessings that are right here in this moment. I trust that Your grace is sufficient for this day, and each day that follows.

❧

My sheep hear my voice, and I know them, and they follow Me.

JOHN 10:27

Knowing How to Pack
for the Wilderness

*L*ord, I know that it is not *where* we are in life that matters, but *Who* is with us. So whenever I have to step out of my comfort zone, or leave behind what is familiar to me to step into what is unfamiliar, I will take my comfort knowing You are with me and will never leave me or forsake me. Thank You that You have provided for my needs in the past and will continue to provide for me in the future, as You have promised in Your Word.

Ask, and it will be given to you; seek, and you will find; knock, and it will be opened to you. For everyone who asks receives, and he who seeks finds, and to him who knocks it will be opened.

MATTHEW 7:7-8

Knowing How to Pack
for the Wilderness

*L*ord, if You call me into a wilderness experience, I will embrace it because I know that You will be there with me. Open my eyes to all the blessings You have for me in every moment of it. Whatever I need to lay down or forsake, help me to willingly and joyfully do so. I want to feel the solid ground at the center of Your perfect will. I don't want to grumble like the Israelites did and end up wandering around for years. I want to learn what You have to teach me so I can move on into all You have for me.

When He had called the people to Himself, with His disciples also, He said to them, "Whoever desires to come after Me, let him deny himself, and take up his cross, and follow Me."

MARK 8:34

Surrendering Your Dreams

*L*ord, I release all my hopes and dreams to You this day. If there is anything that I am longing for that is not to be a part of my life, I ask You to take away the desire for it so that what *should* be in my life will be released to me. I realize how dangerous it is to make idols of my dreams—to try and force my life to be what I have envisioned for myself. I lift up to you all that I desire, and I declare this day that I desire *You* more. I want the desires of my heart to line up with the desires of *Your* heart.

Delight yourself also in the LORD, and He shall give you the desires of your heart.

PSALM 37:4

Surrendering Your Dreams

*L*ord, I know that You have put dreams in my heart for Your purposes. And I know You want me to have a vision for my future. But I know, too, that in my dreaming and envisioning You don't want me to exclude You. So I surrender to You all my dreams and ask You to give me a vision for my future.

Where there is no vision, the people perish.

PROVERBS 29:18 KJV

Surrendering Your Dreams

$\mathcal{L}$ord, as hard as it is for me to let go of the hopes and dreams I have for my life, I lay them all at Your feet. I know that as I die to them, You will either bury them forever or resurrect them to life. I accept Your decision and fully submit to it. Lead me in Your path, Lord. I don't want to speak a vision of my own heart (Jeremiah 23:16). You never said life would be easy. You said You would be with me. I now take each step with the light of Your presence as my guide.

I will rejoice in the LORD, I will joy in the God of my salvation. The LORD God is my strength; He will make my feet like deer's feet, and He will make me walk on my high hills.

HABAKKUK 3:18-19

Surrendering Your Dreams

*L*ord, the greatest dream I have for my life and the deepest desire of my heart is (name your greatest dream). I surrender that dream into Your hands this day. Take the desire for it out of my mind and heart if it is not of You, and help me to die to it completely. If it is Your will for me, I trust You to resurrect my hope and make the dream happen in Your perfect timing. I give You all the gifts and talents You have put in me and ask that You would use them for Your glory. I rest in the joy and peace of knowing my life is in Your hands.

Blessed be the LORD, because He has heard the voice of my supplications! The LORD is my strength and my shield; my heart trusted in Him, and I am helped; therefore my heart greatly rejoices, and with my song I will praise Him.

PSALM 28:6-7

Waiting in the Wings

*L*ord, I wait upon You this day. I put my hope in Your Word and ask that You would fill me afresh with Your Holy Spirit and wash away all anxiety and doubt. I don't want my impatience or lack of trust to stand in the way of all You desire to do in me. I realize that even when my life seems to be standing still, as long as I cling to You I am moving forward on the path You have for me.

The LORD is good to those who wait for Him, to the soul who seeks Him. It is good that one should hope and wait quietly for the salvation of the LORD.

LAMENTATIONS 3:25-26

Waiting in the Wings

*L*ord, as I wait on You, help me to grow in my understanding of Your ways and not succumb to impatience or discouragement because my timetable does not coincide with Yours. Shine Your light into any dark corner of my soul that needs to be exposed. Strengthen my faith to depend on Your perfect timing for my life. Help me to rest in You and be content with the step I'm on and the light You have given me.

I wait for the LORD, my soul waits, and in His Word I do hope. My soul waits for the LORD more than those who watch for the morning.

PSALM 130:5-6

Waiting in the Wings

*L*ord, I choose to wait on You instead of just waiting for things to happen. I refuse to run ahead of Your perfect will for my life. At the same time, I don't want to lag behind it either because of steps I have neglected to take. Show me where I have not been diligent to do things You want me to do. I commit to trusting Your Word and delighting myself in You. I rest in You this day and wait patiently for You to bring to pass all that needs to happen in my life. Bless me with patience in the process.

Wait on the LORD; be of good courage, and He shall strengthen your heart; wait, I say, on the LORD!

PSALM 27:14

Expecting a Call

*L*ord, I know You have great purpose for me and a plan for my life. Open my ears to hear Your voice leading me into all You have for me. Align my heart with Yours and prepare me to understand where You would have me to go and what You would have me to do. Help me to hear Your call. If my expectations and plans are out of alignment with Your will for me, I surrender them to You. I let my desires for myself die. I would rather endure the suffering of that than the pain of never realizing what You made me to be.

You are a chosen generation, a royal priesthood, a holy nation, His own special people, that you may proclaim the praises of Him who called you out of darkness into His marvelous light.

1 PETER 2:9

Expecting a Call

*L*ord, I exalt You above all things. May Your kingdom come this day and Your will be done on earth as it is in heaven. Help me to embrace the calling You have for me. Show me what it is You want me to do and the timing of when You want me to do it. I know that You have a high purpose for my life. Enable me to be a great ambassador for Your kingdom. May people love You more because of what they see of You in me. Only by the power of Your Spirit can this be accomplished.

We have this treasure in earthen vessels, that the excellence of the power may be of God and not of us.

2 CORINTHIANS 4:7

Expecting a Call

*L*ord, because I want to hear Your voice say, "Well done, My good and faithful servant," when I meet You face to face, I want to make sure that I carefully listen to Your voice now. I don't want to be unfruitful and unfulfilled because I never clearly heard Your call. I want You to fill me with Your greatness so that I may do great things for others as You have called me to do. I commit to walking this road step by step with You so that I may fully become all that You have made me to be.

Everyone who is called by My name, whom I have created for My glory; I have formed him, yes, I have made him.

ISAIAH 43:7

Expecting a Call

*L*ord, I know that Your call upon my life includes being a servant, obeying Your commandments, and always growing as a worshiper. Help me to do all of these things according to Your will. Show me where I am failing to do them as fully as You would like. I know I have been called out of darkness to proclaim Your praises. So I proclaim them this day and say all praise be to You, O Lord of heaven and earth.

Moreover whom He predestined, these He also called; whom He called, these He also justified; and whom He justified, these He also glorified.

ROMANS 8:30

Believing It's Not Over
Till It's Over

*L*ord, my times are in Your hands. Thank You that my life is never over here on this earth until You say it is. And when that time comes, I will see You face to face and dwell in Your presence. Thank You that You never give up on me, even when I have given up on myself. I am so happy that no matter what age I am, I will always have purpose because You have great things for me to do.

Those who are planted in the house of the LORD shall flourish in the courts of our God. They shall still bear fruit in old age; they shall be fresh and flourishing.

PSALM 92:13-14

Believing It's Not Over Till It's Over

*L*ord, I know from Your Word that You never put us out to pasture because we have outlived our usefulness and purpose. Thank You that Your call on my life will continue until I go to be with You. But I also know that the specific details of how my purpose on earth is lived out can change. Help me to always hear Your voice leading me in the way I should go.

You will show me the path of life; in Your presence is the fullness of joy; at Your right hand are pleasures forevermore.

PSALM 16:11

Believing It's Not Over
Till It's Over

*L*ord, when it's time for me to do something different, help me not to cling to the past or be afraid to move into the future You have for me. Your Word says that Your plans for me are for good, and I know that I am secure as long as I walk through each day with You. Give me strength, courage, health, wisdom, revelation, and faith for the journey. I trust You to keep me on the right path and to continue giving me the light I need for the step I'm on.

Listen to counsel and receive instruction, that you may be wise in your latter days.

PROVERBS 19:20

Believing It's Not Over
Till It's Over

❧

*L*ord, I know that fruit is seasonal and that I won't necessarily be bearing fruit constantly. When I am in a season of rest so that the soil of my life won't be depleted, help me not to worry that my life is over. Help me not to strive against what is to be a time of preparing the soil of my heart for what is to come. Thank You that You will always produce a fresh crop through me as long as I am willing to be planted.

❧

Not by might nor by power, but by my Spirit, says the LORD of Hosts.

ZECHARIAH 4:6

Believing It's Not Over Till It's Over

❧

*L*ord, I pray that You would give me an ever-renewing sense of Your purpose for my life. Use me for Your glory as long as I am on this earth. Help me to never be resistant to change, but instead to always be open to new things You want to do in my life. I don't want to hang on to the old life when You are wanting to make a new beginning. Help me to always be in Your Word, in close communication with You, and seeking only the counsel of godly people so that I will never miss Your light shining on the path You have for me.

❧

Show me Your ways, O LORD; teach me Your paths. Lead me in Your truth and teach me, for You are the God of my salvation; on You I wait all the day.

PSALM 25:4-5

Surviving Disappointment

⤞⤟⤠

*L*ord, You alone are my guide, my companion, my strength, and my life. I need no other to fulfill my expectations, for all my hopes and expectations are in You. Show me what You want me to see. I refuse to allow disappointment to color my mind and emotions and outlook. I put You in charge of every detail of my life, even the pain I feel in my heart. Use it to perfect me and bring glory to You. Thank You for Your endless goodness toward me. I lift my hands to You, and I trust that the light I have is sufficient for what I face this day and this moment.

⤞⤟⤠

They cried to you and were saved; in you they trusted and were not disappointed.

PSALM 22:5 NIV

Surviving Disappointment

*L*ord, I know that times of disappointment are inevitable because life can't always live up to our expectations. But when someone or some situation fails me, or I fail myself, help me to remember to put my expectations in You. Help me to remember that the happiness and fulfillment I experience in life don't depend on other people or situations, they depend on You. You are all I need in every situation.

When I fall, I will arise; when I sit in darkness, the Lord will be a light to me.

MICAH 7:8

Surviving Disappointment

*L*ord, in times of great disappointment I will cling to You. As I walk through those times, teach me what You want me to learn. Reveal Your truth to me in every situation. Help me to see it clearly for what it really is. Keep me from fretting over my circumstances or living in unforgiveness regarding them. I want to, instead, wait in Your presence for You to reveal Your goodness to me in the situation. I want to always rest in You, knowing my life is in Your hands.

My soul, wait silently for God alone, for my expectation is from Him.

PSALM 62:5

Traveling Through the Dark Moments of Relationships

*L*ord, I give all my relationships to You and ask that You be in charge of them. May Your spirit of unity reign in each one. If any are not of You, take them out of my life. Concerning my relationship with (_____), I ask that Your spirit of love and peace would reign between us. Lead him (her) in the way You would have him (her) to go. Bless him (her) and help him (her) to have a closer walk with You. Guide us both through any difficult times and help us to discern clearly the hand of the enemy when he comes to lie and destroy.

If we walk in the light as He is in the light, we have fellowship with one another, and the blood of Jesus Christ His Son cleanses us from all sin.

1 JOHN 1:7

Traveling Through the Dark Moments of Relationships

*L*ord, show me anyone I have not forgiven so that I can confess that unforgiveness to You as sin. Specifically, I pray about my relationship with (name anyone you need to forgive). Bring reconciliation between us. Help me to humble myself before that person and put their need first so that wounds can be healed and the relationship can be restored.

First be reconciled to your brother, and then come and offer your gift.

MATTHEW 5:24

Traveling Through the Dark Moments of Relationships

*L*ord, shine Your light of revelation into every relationship I have and show me Your truth. Illuminate any darkness of unforgiveness in me, and I will confess it to You as sin. Bring reconciliation and clarity in place of misunderstanding. Where I need to humbly extend myself, enable me to make any necessary sacrifice and not cater to the cries of my flesh. Help me to lay down my life in prayer for my family, friends, and others You have put in my life. Teach me how to love the way that You do. I join my hand in Yours as I travel the path of relationships with Your unconditional love as my guiding light.

Be kind to one another, tenderhearted, forgiving one another, even as God in Christ forgave you.

EPHESIANS 4:31-32

Traveling Through the Dark Moments of Relationships

*L*ord, I release all my relationships to You. Help me not to hold on to them too tightly, but instead to hold tightly to You. I know that the enemy wants to create strife and discord in my relationships, so I ask that You would be in charge of every one that I have. Help me to be humble, considerate, compassionate, and loving toward each person. Enable me to make the sacrifices I need to make for others as You reveal their needs to me. Help me to be unselfish as I look out for the interests of others.

Let nothing be done through selfish ambition or conceit, but in lowliness of mind let each esteem others better than himself. Let each of you look out not only for his own interests, but also for the interests of others.

PHILIPPIANS 2:3-4

Walking in the Midst of the Overwhelming

*L*ord, while there are many things that can happen in life that are frightening or overwhelming, I know that Your power is greater than all of them. Even when what I experience is too much for me, it is never too much for You. Anything I face is nothing alongside Your ability to redeem it. Lord, I lift to You the things that frighten me most and ask that You would protect me and the people I love from them. Specifically, I bring before You (name of overwhelming situation) and ask that You would work Your redemption in it.

Hear my cry, O God; attend to my prayer. From the end of the earth I will cry to You, when my heart is overwhelmed; lead me to the rock that is higher than I.

PSALM 61:1-2

Walking in the Midst of the Overwhelming

*L*ord, whatever I need to do to make my path one of safety and peace, show me how and enable me to do it. Give me wisdom, strength, and clarity of mind to hear what You are saying to me in the midst of any dark or overwhelming situation. I know that it is my enemy who "has made me dwell in darkness. Therefore my spirit is overwhelmed within me. Cause me to know the way in which I should walk, for I lift up my soul to You" (Psalm 143:3-4,8). May my life be a testimony of the power of Your glory manifested as I walk in the light You have given me.

The LORD is my light and my salvation; whom shall I fear? The LORD is the strength of my life; of whom shall I be afraid?

PSALM 27:1

Walking in the Midst of the Overwhelming

∼≈≋≈∼

*L*ord, I ask that You would send one or more persons into my life who are willing to pray with me on a regular basis. Let them be people who are trustworthy and mature in Your ways, and who have faith to believe for answers to prayer. Help me be sensitive as to who they might be. I know that when the things I face seem overwhelming, I need the prayer support of people of strong faith. Enable me to be bold enough to ask for their prayer support.

∼≈∼

If you have faith as a mustard seed, you can say to this mulberry tree, "Be pulled up by the roots and be planted in the sea," and it would obey you.

LUKE 17:6

Walking in the Midst of the Overwhelming

*L*ord, help me to recognize anything that seems overwhelming to me as a sign that I need to immediately draw close to You and pray. Give me a clear sense of what is going on and show me exactly how to pray about it. I know that Your perfect love will take away all my fear. Perfect me in Your love so that I don't fall victim to the torment that fear can bring. Give me a deeper sense of Your presence, for I know that Your presence is far greater than anything that overwhelms me.

There is no fear in love; but perfect love casts out fear, because fear involves torment. But he who fears has not been made perfect in love.

1 JOHN 4:18

Reaching for God's Hand
in Times of Loss

*L*ord, only You can fill the empty places in the canyon of sorrow that has been left in my heart because of losses I have experienced. Thank You that You are the one constant in my life that can never be lost to me. All else is temporary and changing. I know You are a good God and Your love for me is endless. Help me to cast my whole burden of grief on You and let You carry it. Even though there will be times when it feels like I can't live through the pain, I know You will sustain me.

The people who walked in darkness have seen a great light; those who dwelt in the land of the shadow of death, upon them a light has shined.

ISAIAH 9:2

Reaching for God's Hand
in Times of Loss

*L*ord, enable me to get beyond any sorrow or grief I feel in my life. I realize life must go on, and I ask You to help me take the next step I need to take today. Even though it may be hard to imagine life without the pain I feel, with You all things are possible. Your healing power can restore anything—even a broken heart. Walk with me, Lord. I trust You to take my hand and lead me until I can feel Your light on my face and joy in my heart once again.

Remember the word to Your servant, upon which You have caused me to hope. This is my comfort in my affliction, for Your word has given me life.

PSALM 119:49-50

Reaching for God's Hand in Times of Loss

*L*ord, I pray that You would heal me of any grief I carry in my heart. I know that no matter how dark the situation around me seems, Your light in me can never be put out. I know that Your Word says that no matter how great the loss, there will be a time when my grief will end. I thank you for that.

The LORD will be your everlasting light, and the days of your mourning shall be ended.

ISAIAH 60:20

Reaching for God's Hand in Times of Loss

*L*ord, where I have experienced loss in the past and still carry grief in my heart, I pray that You would take it away. I want to walk with You as You carry this burden for me. If I have not grieved properly, help me to cry every tear that needs to be shed in order for full release to come to my soul. If I have harbored any unforgiveness, bitterness, or resentment, I confess that as a sin before You and ask You to deliver me from these debilitating emotions. Thank You for Your comfort to me in my time of mourning.

Blessed are those who mourn, for they shall be comforted.

MATTHEW 5:4

Stepping Out
of the Past

*L*ord, I release my past to You. I give You my bad memories and ask that You would heal me to complete wholeness so that they no longer hurt, torment, or control me. Bring me to the point where my past, even as recent as yesterday, will in no way negatively affect today. I give You my past failures in the area of (name any recurring problem). Set me free from this. Even though I may be unable to completely resist the pull of certain things on my own, I know You are able to set me free. Make me a testimony to the power of Your healing and deliverance.

Therefore, if anyone is in Christ, he is a new creation; old things have passed away; behold, all things have become new.

2 CORINTHIANS 5:17

Stepping Out
of the Past

*L*ord, I confess any unforgiveness in my heart for things that have happened in the past, and I release all persons who are associated with it. I specifically forgive (name of person I need to forgive). Lord, heal all misunderstandings or hurts that have happened between us. I know that I can never be free and healed if I tie myself to others by unforgiveness, so I ask You to bring to light any unforgiveness in me of which I'm not even aware. Give me Your revelation and show me all I need to see in order to walk out of the shadow of my past and into the light You have for me today.

Forget the former things; do not dwell in the past. See, I am doing a new thing! Now it springs up; do you not perceive it? I am making a way in the desert and streams in the wasteland.

ISAIAH 43:18-19 NIV

Stepping Out
of the Past

～～～

$\mathcal{L}$ord, help me to be renewed in the spirit of my mind. Where I have made wrong choices in the past, I pray that You would forgive me and redeem those mistakes. Help me to forgive myself so that I don't keep replaying them in my thoughts. Take all of my past failures and use them for good today. I know that because I have put You in charge of my future, I don't have to fear that the events of my past will keep me from moving into all You have for me.

～～～

That you put off, concerning your former conduct, the old man which grows corrupt according to the deceitful lusts, and be renewed in the spirit of your mind, and that you put on the new man which was created according to God, in true righteousness and holiness.

EPHESIANS 4:22-24

Maintaining a Passion for the Present

$\mathcal{L}$ord, I want to live my life the way You want me to every day. Help me not to be stuck in my past, or so geared toward the future that I miss the richness of the present. Help me to experience the wealth in each moment. I don't desire to take a single step apart from Your presence. If You're not moving me, I'm staying here until I have a leading from You. I know I can only get to the future You have for me by walking one step at a time in Your will today. Help me to not walk in darkness, but always in Your marvelous light.

The night is far spent, the day is at hand. Therefore let us cast off the works of darkness, and let us put on the armor of light.

ROMANS 13:12

Maintaining a Passion for the Present

*L*ord, I realize there is no better time than the present to be Your light extended to those around me. Help me to get beyond myself and become an open vessel through which Your light can shine. Give me Your wisdom and revelation, and show me all I need to see to keep me on the road You have for me. Enable me to step out of my past and keep an eye on the future by following Your light on my path today.

Let your light so shine before men, that they may see your good works and glorify your Father in heaven.

MATTHEW 5:16

Maintaining a Passion for the Present

*L*ord, I know that You have not made me to live in anxiety about anything. Thank You that, instead, I can bring my concerns to You and exchange them for Your peace which passes all understanding. Help me to never dwell on my suffering, for I know that it is nothing compared to the glory set before me when I walk through it with You. I reach out my hand to You this day so that I can walk safely in Your shadow.

For I consider that the sufferings of this present time are not worthy to be compared with the glory which shall be revealed in us.

ROMANS 8:18

Moving into Your Future

*L*ord, I ask You to be in charge of my future. I don't want to dream dreams if You are not in them. I don't want to make plans that You will not bless. I don't want to work hard trying to harvest something that will never bear fruit because I did not receive the seed from You. Help me not to waste valuable time getting off the path and having to come back to the same place again. I don't want to get to the end of my life and regret the time I spent not living for You.

Mark the blameless man, and observe the upright; for the future of that man is peace.

PSALM 37:37

Moving into
Your Future

⟡

*L*ord, where I have made the mistake of doing what I want and then expecting You to bless it, forgive me. Instead I ask what You want me to do, knowing that when I do Your will, You will bless me. Enable me to hear Your voice and trust Your leading. I want it said of me when I leave this earth and go to be with You, that I walked with God. I want it said that Your glory was seen in my life. I trust my future to You, knowing You have it safely in Your hands.

⟡

Arise, shine; for your light has come! And the glory of the LORD is risen upon you. For behold, the darkness shall cover the earth, and deep darkness the people; but the LORD will arise over you, and His glory will be seen upon you.

ISAIAH 60:1-2

Moving into Your Future

*L*ord, I surrender my past, present, and future to You now. Help me not to be anxious about my future but to rest in the knowledge that my future is secure in You. I want to keep one foot in eternity by never letting go of Your hand. I want to store up so many treasures in heaven that heaven will feel familiar the moment I arrive. And when I do take that final step into my eternal future with You, I trust that You will be there for me with all the light I need for that step, too.

There is surely a future hope for you, and your hope will not be cut off.

PROVERBS 23:18 NIV

PART IV

The Power *of a* PRAYING WIFE

His Wife

*L*ord, help me to be a good wife. I fully realize that I don't have what it takes to be one without Your help.

Take my selfishness, impatience, and irritability and turn them into kindness, long-suffering, and the willingness to bear all things.

Take my old emotional habits, mindsets, automatic reactions, rude assumptions, and self-protectiveness, and make me patient, kind, good, faithful, gentle, and self-controlled.

Take the hardness of my heart and break down the walls with Your battering ram of revelation. Give me a new heart and work in me Your love, peace, and joy (Galatians 5:22-23). I am not able to rise above who I am at this moment. Only You can transform me.

Whatever things you ask when you pray, believe that you receive them, and you will have them. And whenever you stand praying, if you have anything against anyone, forgive him, that your Father in heaven may also forgive you your trespasses.

MARK 11:24-25

His Wife

*L*ord, I confess the times I've been unloving, critical, angry, resentful, disrespectful, or unforgiving toward my husband.

Help me to put aside any hurt, anger, or disappointment I feel and forgive him the way You do totally and completely, no looking back. Make me a tool of reconciliation, peace, and healing in this marriage. Make me my husband's helpmate, companion, champion, friend, and support.

Help me to create a peaceful, restful, safe place for him to come home to. Teach me how to take care of myself and stay attractive to him. Grow me into a creative and confident woman who is rich in mind, soul, and spirit. Make me the kind of woman he can be proud to say is his wife.

Through wisdom a house is built, and by understanding it is established; by knowledge the rooms are filled with all precious and pleasant riches.

PROVERBS 24:3-4

His Wife

*L*ord, I lay all my expectations at Your cross. I release my husband from the burden of fulfilling me in areas where I should be looking to You.

Help me to accept him the way he is and not try to change him. I realize that in some ways he may never change, but at the same time, I release him to change in ways I never thought he could.

I leave any changing that needs to be done in Your hands, fully accepting that neither of us is perfect and never will be.

Only You, Lord, are perfect, and I look to You to perfect us. May we be perfectly joined together in the same mind and in the same judgment (1 Corinthians 1:10).

Be kind to one another, tenderhearted, forgiving one another, even as God in Christ forgave you.

EPHESIANS 4:32

His Wife

*L*ord, teach me how to pray for my husband and make my prayers a true language of love. Where love has died, create new love between us. Show me what unconditional love really is and how to communicate it in a way he can clearly perceive.

Bring unity between us so that we can be in agreement about everything (Amos 3:3). May the God of patience and comfort grant us to be like-minded toward one another, according to Christ Jesus (Romans 15:5).

Make us a team, not pursuing separate, competitive, or independent lives, but working together, overlooking each other's faults and weaknesses for the greater good of the marriage. Help us to pursue the things which make for peace and the things by which one may edify another (Romans 14:19).

Let us not grow weary while doing good, for in due season we shall reap if we do not lose heart.

GALATIANS 6:9

His Wife

*L*ord, I pray that the commitment my husband and I have to You and to one another will grow stronger and more passionate every day. Enable him to be the head of the home as You made him to be, and show me how to support and respect him as he rises to that place of leadership.

Reveal to me what he wants and needs and show me potential problems before they arise. Breathe Your life into this marriage. Make me a new person, Lord. Give me a fresh perspective, a positive outlook, and a renewed relationship with the man You've given me.

Help me see him with new eyes, new appreciation, new love, new compassion, and new acceptance. Give my husband a new wife, and let it be me.

Ask, and it will be given to you; seek, and you will find; knock, and it will be opened to you. For everyone who asks receives, and he who seeks finds, and to him who knocks it will be opened.

MATTHEW 7:7-8

His Work

*L*ord, I pray that You would bless the work of my husband's hands. May his labor bring not only favor, success, and prosperity, but great fulfillment as well. If the work he is doing is not in line with Your perfect will for his life, reveal it to him. Show him what he should do differently and guide him down the right path.

Give him strength, faith, and a vision for the future so he can rise above any propensity for laziness. May he never run from work out of fear, selfishness, or a desire to avoid responsibility.

On the other hand, help him to see that he doesn't have to work himself to death for man's approval. Give him the ability to enjoy his success without striving for more. Help him to excel, but free him from the pressure to do so.

Do you see a man who excels in his work? He will stand before kings; he will not stand before unknown men.

PROVERBS 22:29

His Work

*G*od, I pray that You will be Lord over my husband's work. May he bring You into every aspect of it. Give him enough confidence in the gifts You've placed in him to be able to seek, find, and do good work. Open up doors of opportunity for him that no man can close.

Develop his skills so that they grow more valuable with each passing year. Show me what I can do to encourage him. I pray that his work will be established, secure, successful, satisfying, and financially rewarding.

Let him be like a tree planted by the stream of Your living water, which brings forth fruit in due season. May he never wither under pressure, but grow strong and prosper (Psalm 1:3).

Let the beauty of the LORD our God be upon us, and establish the work of our hands for us; yes, establish the work of our hands.

PSALM 90:17

His Finances

*L*ord, I commit our finances to You. Be in charge of them and use them for Your purposes.

May my husband and I be good stewards of all that You give us and walk in total agreement as to how it is to be disbursed. I pray that we will learn to live free of burdensome debt.

Where we have not been wise, bring restoration and give us guidance. Show me how I can help increase our finances and not decrease them unwisely. Help us to remember that all we have belongs to You and to be grateful for it.

Do not seek what you should eat or what you should drink, nor have an anxious mind. For all these things the nations of the world seek after, and your Father knows that you need these things. But seek the kingdom of God, and all these things shall be added to you.

LUKE 12:29-31

His Finances

*L*ord, I pray that (husband's name) will have wisdom to handle money wisely. Help him make good decisions as to how he spends. Show him how to plan for the future. Teach him to give as You have instructed in Your Word.

I pray that he will find the perfect balance between spending needlessly and being miserly. May he always be paid well for the work he does, and may his money not be stolen, lost, devoured, destroyed, or wasted. Multiply it so that what he makes will go a long way.

I pray that he will not be anxious about finances, but will seek Your kingdom first, knowing that as he does, we will have all we need (Luke 12:31).

My God shall supply all your need according to His riches in glory by Christ Jesus.

PHILIPPIANS 4:19

His Sexuality

*L*ord, bless my husband's sexuality and make it an area of great fulfillment for him.

I pray that we make time for one another, communicate our true feelings openly, and remain sensitive to what each other needs. Keep us sexually pure in mind and body, and close the door to anything lustful or illicit that seeks to encroach upon us.

Deliver us from the bondage of past mistakes. Remove completely the effect of any sexual experience in thought or deed that has ever happened to us outside of our relationship. Purify us by the power of Your Spirit.

Flee sexual immorality. Every sin that a man does is outside the body, but he who commits sexual immorality sins against his own body. Or do you not know that your body is the temple of the Holy Spirit who is in you, whom you have from God, and you are not your own? For you were bought at a price; therefore glorify God in your body and in your spirit, which are God's.

1 CORINTHIANS 6:18-20

His Sexuality

*L*ord, take away anyone or anything from my husband's life that would inspire temptation to infidelity. Help him to abstain from sexual immorality so that he will know how to possess his own vessel in sanctification and honor (1 Thessalonians 4:3-4).

I pray that we will desire each other and no one else. Show me how to make myself attractive and desirable to him and be the kind of partner he needs. I pray that neither of us will ever be tempted to think about seeking fulfillment elsewhere. I realize that an important part of my ministry to my husband is sexual. Help me to never use it as a weapon or a means of manipulation by giving and withholding it for selfish reasons.

I commit this area of our lives to You, Lord. May it be continually new and alive. Make it all that You created it to be.

The body is not for sexual immorality but for the Lord, and the Lord for the body.

1 CORINTHIANS 6:13

His Affection

*L*ord, I pray for open physical affection between my husband and me. Enable each of us to lay aside self-consciousness or apathy and be effusive in our display of love. Help us to demonstrate how much we care for and value each other.

Help us to not be cold, undemonstrative, uninterested, or remote. Enable us to be warm, tender, compassionate, loving, and adoring. Break through any hardheadedness on our part that refuses to change and grow. If one of us is less affectionate to the other's detriment, bring us into balance.

Change our habits of indifference so that we can become the husband and wife You called us to be.

So husbands ought to love their own wives as their own bodies; he who loves his wife loves himself. For no one ever hated his own flesh, but nourishes and cherishes it, just as the Lord does the church.

EPHESIANS 5:28-29

His Temptations

Lord, I pray that You would strengthen my husband to resist any temptation that comes his way. Remove temptation especially in the area of (name of specific temptation).

Make him strong where he is weak. Help him to rise above anything that seeks to erect a stronghold in his life. Lord, You've said that whoever has no rule over his own spirit is like a city broken down, without walls (Proverbs 25:28).

I pray that (husband's name) will not be broken down by the power of evil, but raised up by the power of God. Help him to take charge over his own spirit and have self-control to resist anything and anyone who becomes a temptation.

No temptation has overtaken you except such as is common to man; but God is faithful, who will not allow you to be tempted beyond what you are able, but with the temptation will also make the way of escape, that you may be able to bear it.

1 CORINTHIANS 10:13

His Mind

*L*ord, I pray for Your protection on my husband's mind. Shield him from the lies of the enemy. Help him to clearly discern between Your voice and any other, and show him how to take every thought captive as You have instructed us to do.

May he thirst for Your Word and hunger for Your truth so that he can recognize wrong thinking. Lord, You have given me authority over all the power of the enemy (Luke 10:19). By that authority given to me in Jesus Christ, I command any lying spirits away from my husband's mind. I proclaim that You, God, have given (husband's name) a sound mind.

Though we walk in the flesh, we do not war according to the flesh. For the weapons of our warfare are not carnal but mighty in God for pulling down strongholds, casting down arguments and every high thing that exalts itself against the knowledge of God, bringing every thought into captivity to the obedience of Christ.

2 CORINTHIANS 10:3-5

His Mind

*L*ord, I pray that my husband will not entertain confusion in his mind, but will live in clarity. Keep him from being tormented with impure, evil, negative, or sinful thoughts. Enable him to be transformed by the renewing of his mind (Romans 12:2).

Help him to be anxious for nothing, but in everything by prayer and supplication, with thanksgiving, let his requests be made known to You; and may Your peace, which surpasses all understanding, guard his heart and mind through Christ Jesus (Philippians 4:6-7).

And finally, whatever things are true, noble, just, pure, lovely, of good report, having virtue, or anything praiseworthy, let him think on these things (Philippians 4:8).

To be carnally minded is death, but to be spiritually minded is life and peace.

ROMANS 8:6

His Fears

Lord, You've said in Your Word that there is no fear in love; but perfect love casts out fear, because fear involves torment. But he who fears has not been made perfect in love (1 John 4:18).

I pray You will perfect my husband in Your love so that tormenting fear finds no place in him. I know You have not given him a spirit of fear. You've given him power, love, and a sound mind (2 Timothy 1:7).

I pray in the name of Jesus that fear will not rule over my husband. Instead, may Your Word penetrate every fiber of his being, convincing him that Your love for him is far greater than anything he faces and nothing can separate him from it.

The angel of the LORD encamps all around those who fear Him, and delivers them.

PSALM 34:7

His Fears

*L*ord, I pray that my husband will acknowledge You as a Father whose love is unfailing, whose strength is without equal, and in whose presence there is nothing to fear. Deliver him this day from fear that destroys and replace it with godly fear (Jeremiah 32:40).

Teach him Your way, O Lord. Help him to walk in Your truth. Unite his heart to fear Your name (Psalm 86:11).

May he have no fear of men, but rise up and boldly say, The Lord is my helper; I will not fear. What can man do to me? (Hebrews 13:6). How great is Your goodness, which You have laid up for those who fear You (Psalm 31:19).

Fear not, for I am with you; be not dismayed, for I am your God. I will strengthen you, yes, I will help you, I will uphold you with My righteous right hand.

ISAIAH 41:10

His Fears

I say to you, (husband's name), Be strong, do not fear! Behold, your God will come with vengeance, with the recompense of God; He will come and save you (Isaiah 35:4).

In righteousness you shall be established; you shall be far from oppression, for you shall not fear (Isaiah 54:14).

You shall not be afraid of the terror by night, nor of the arrow that flies by day, nor of the pestilence that walks in darkness, nor of the destruction that lays waste at noonday (Psalm 91:5-6).

May the Spirit of the Lord rest upon you, the Spirit of wisdom and understanding, the Spirit of counsel and might, the Spirit of knowledge and of the fear of the Lord (Isaiah 11:2).

I sought the LORD, and He heard me, and delivered me from all my fears.

PSALM 34:4

His Purpose

$\mathcal{L}$ord, I pray that (husband's name) will clearly hear the call You have on his life. Help him to realize who he is in Christ and give him certainty he was created for a high purpose. Enable him to walk worthy of his calling and remind him of what You've called him to be.

Strike down discouragement so that it will not defeat him. Lift his eyes above the circumstances of the moment so he can see the purpose for which You created him. Give him patience to wait for Your perfect timing.

I pray that the desires of his heart will not be in conflict with the desires of Yours. May he seek You for direction and hear when You speak to his soul.

The God of our Lord Jesus Christ, the Father of glory, may give to you the spirit of wisdom and revelation in the knowledge of Him, the eyes of your understanding being enlightened; that you may know what is the hope of His calling, what are the riches of the glory of His inheritance in the saints.

EPHESIANS 1:17-18

His Choices

*L*ord, fill my husband with the fear of the Lord and give him wisdom for every decision he makes. May he reverence You and Your ways and seek to know Your truth. Give him discernment to make decisions based on Your revelation. Help him to make godly choices and keep him from doing anything foolish.

I pray that he will listen to godly counselors and not be a man who is unteachable. Instruct him even as he is sleeping (Psalm 16:7), and in the morning, I pray he will do what's right rather than follow the leading of his own flesh. May he not buy into the foolishness of this world, but keep his eyes on You and have ears to hear Your voice.

A wise man will hear and increase learning, and a man of understanding will attain wise counsel.

PROVERBS 1:5

His Health

*L*ord, I pray for Your healing touch on (husband's name). Make every part of his body function the way You designed it to.

Wherever there is anything out of balance, set it in perfect working order. Heal him of any disease, illness, injury, infirmity, or weakness.

Strengthen his body to successfully endure his workload, and when he sleeps may he wake up completely rested, rejuvenated, and refreshed.

I pray that he will have the desire to take care of his body, to eat the kind of food that brings health, to get regular exercise, and avoid anything that would be harmful to him. Help him to understand that his body is Your temple and he should care for it as such (1 Corinthians 3:16).

I have heard your prayer, I have seen your tears; surely I will heal you.

2 KINGS 20:5

His Health

$\mathscr{L}$ord, I pray that You will give my husband a strong heart that doesn't fail. When he is ill, I pray You will sustain him and heal him. Fill him with Your joy to give him strength.

Specifically, I pray for (mention any area of concern). Give him faith to say, O Lord my God, I cried out to You, and You healed me (Psalm 30:2). Thank You, Lord, that You are his Healer. I pray that my husband will live a long and healthy life and when death does come, may it be accompanied by peace and not unbearable suffering and agony.

Thank You, Lord, that You will be there to welcome him into Your presence, and not a moment before Your appointed hour.

They cried out to the LORD in their trouble, and He saved them out of their distresses. He sent His word and healed them, and delivered them from their destructions.

PSALM 107:19-20

His Protection

*L*ord, I pray that You would protect (husband's name) from any accidents, diseases, dangers, or evil influences. Keep him safe, especially in cars and planes. Hide him from violence and the plans of evil people. Wherever he walks, secure his steps. Keep him on Your path so that his feet don't slip (Psalm 17:5).

If his foot does slip, hold him up by Your mercy (Psalm 94:18). Give him the wisdom and discretion that will help him walk safely and not fall into danger (Proverbs 3:21-23).

Save him from any plans of the enemy that seek to destroy his life (Psalm 103:4). Preserve his going out and his coming in from this time forth and even forevermore (Psalm 121:8).

He who dwells in the secret place of the Most High shall abide under the shadow of the Almighty. I will say to the LORD, He is my refuge and my fortress; my God, in Him I will trust.

PSALM 91:1-2

His Trials

*L*ord, You alone know the depth of the burden my husband carries. I may understand the specifics, but You have measured the weight of it on his shoulders.

I've not come to minimize what You are doing in his life, for I know You work great things in the midst of trials. Nor am I trying to protect him from what he must face.

I only want to support him so that he will get through this battle as the winner. Help him to remember that the steps of a good man are ordered by the Lord, and He delights in his way. Though he fall, he shall not be utterly cast down; for the Lord upholds him with His hand (Psalm 37:23-24).

You have been grieved by various trials, that the genuineness of your faith, being much more precious than gold that perishes, though it is tested by fire, may be found to praise, honor, and glory at the revelation of Jesus Christ.

1 PETER 1:6-7

His Trials

God, You are our refuge and strength, a very present help in trouble (Psalm 46:1). You have invited us to come boldly to the throne of grace, that we may obtain mercy and find grace to help in time of need (Hebrews 4:16).

I come before Your throne and ask for grace for my husband. Strengthen his heart for this battle and give him patience to wait on You (Psalm 27:1-4).

Build him up so that no matter what happens he will be able to stand strong through it. Help him to be always rejoicing in hope, patient in tribulation, continuing steadfastly in prayer (Romans 12:12).

Give him endurance to run the race and not give up, for You have said that a righteous man may fall seven times and rise again (Proverbs 24:16).

You, who have shown me great and severe troubles, shall revive me again, and bring me up again from the depths of the earth. You shall increase my greatness, and comfort me on every side.

PSALM 71:20-21

His Trials

*L*ord, I pray that in the midst of trials my husband will look to You to be his refuge until these calamities have passed by (Psalm 57:1).

May he learn to wait on You because those who wait on the Lord shall renew their strength; they shall mount up with wings like eagles, they shall run and not be weary, they shall walk and not faint (Isaiah 40:31).

I pray that he will find his strength in You and as he cries out to You, You will hear him and save him out of all his troubles (Psalm 34:6).

Teach him to cast his burdens on You and let You sustain him through everything that is happening in his life.

As for me, I will call upon God, and the Lord shall save me. Evening and morning and at noon I will pray, and cry aloud, and He shall hear my voice. He has redeemed my soul in peace from the battle that was against me.

PSALM 55:16-18

His Integrity

*L*ord, I pray that You would make my husband a man of integrity, according to Your standards.

Give him strength to say Yes when he should say Yes and courage to say No when he should say No. Enable him to stand for what he knows is right and not waver under pressure from the world.

Don't let him be a man who is always learning and never able to come to the knowledge of the truth (2 Timothy 3:7).

Give him, instead, a teachable spirit that is willing to listen to the voice of wisdom and grow in Your ways.

The integrity of the upright will guide them, but the perversity of the unfaithful will destroy them.

PROVERBS 11:3

His Integrity

❧❧❧

*L*ord, I pray that You would make my husband a man who lives by truth. Help him to walk with Your Spirit of truth at all times (John 16:13). Be with him to bear witness to the truth so that in times of pressure he will act on it with confidence (1 John 1:8-9).

Where he has erred in this and other matters, give him a heart that is quick to confess his mistakes. For You have said in Your Word, If we say that we have no sin, we deceive ourselves, and the truth is not in us (1 John 1:8).

Don't let him be deceived. Don't let him live a lie in any way. Bind mercy and truth around his neck and write them on the tablet of his heart so he will find favor and high esteem in the sight of God and man (Proverbs 3:3-4).

❧❧

Better is the poor who walks in his integrity than one perverse in his ways, though he be rich.

PROVERBS 28:6

His Reputation

*L*ord, I pray that (husband's name) will have a reputation that is untarnished. I know that a man is often valued by what others say of him (Proverbs 27:21), so I pray that he will be respected in our town and people will speak highly of him.

You've said in Your Word that a curse without cause shall not alight (Proverbs 26:2).

Keep him out of legal entanglements. Protect us from lawsuits and criminal proceedings. Deliver him from his enemies, O God. Defend him from those who rise up to do him harm (Psalm 59:1).

In You, O Lord, we put our trust. Let us never be put to shame (Psalm 71:1).

Hide me from the secret plots of the wicked, from the rebellion of the workers of iniquity, who sharpen their tongue like a sword, and bend their bows to shoot their arrows—bitter words.

PSALM 64:2-3

His Reputation

$\mathcal{L}$ord, Your Word says that a good tree cannot bear bad fruit, nor can a bad tree bear good fruit. Every tree that does not bear good fruit is cut down and thrown into the fire (Matthew 7:18-19).

I pray that my husband will bear good fruit out of the goodness that is within him, and that he will be known by the good that he does.

May the fruits of honesty, trustworthiness, and humility sweeten all his dealings so that his reputation will never be spoiled. Pull him out of any net which has been laid for him (Psalm 31:4).

If You are for us, who can be against us (Romans 8:31)?

Do not let me be ashamed, O LORD, for I have called upon You; let the wicked be ashamed; let them be silent in the grave. Let the lying lips be put to silence, which speak insolent things proudly and contemptuously against the righteous.

PSALM 31:17-18

His Reputation

*L*ord, I pray You would keep my husband safe from the evil of gossiping mouths. Let them be ashamed and brought to confusion who seek to destroy his life; let them be driven backward and brought to dishonor who wish him evil (Psalm 40:14).

May he trust in You and not be afraid of what man can do to him (Psalm 56:11). For You have said whoever believes in You will not be put to shame (Romans 10:11).

Lead him, guide him, and be his mighty fortress and hiding place. May his light so shine before men that they see his good works and glorify You, Lord (Matthew 5:16).

Blessed are you when they revile and persecute you, and say all kinds of evil against you falsely for My sake. Rejoice and be exceedingly glad, for great is your reward in heaven, for so they persecuted the prophets who were before you.

MATTHEW 5:11-12

His Priorities

*L*ord, I pray for my husband's priorities to be in perfect order. Be Lord and Ruler over his heart. Help him to choose a simplicity of life that will allow him to have time alone with You, Lord, a place to be quiet in Your presence every day. Speak to him about making Your Word, prayer, and praise a priority. Enable him to place me and our children in greater prominence in his heart than career, friends, and activities.

I pray he will seek You first and submit his all to You, for when he does I know the other pieces of his life will fit together perfectly.

Help me to properly put my husband before children, work, family, friends, activities, and interests. Show me what I can do right now to demonstrate to him that he has this position in my heart.

Seek first the kingdom of God and His righteousness, and all these things shall be added to you.

MATTHEW 6:33

His Relationships

*L*ord, I pray for (husband's name) to have good, godly male friends with whom he can openly share his heart. May they be trustworthy men of wisdom who will speak truth into his life and not just say what he wants to hear (Proverbs 28:23).

Show him the importance of godly friendships and help me encourage him to sustain them.

I pray for strong, peaceful relationships with each of his family members, neighbors, acquaintances, and coworkers. Today I specifically pray for his relationship with (name of person).

Let there be reconciliation and peace where there has been estrangement.

A new commandment I give to you, that you love one another; as I have loved you, that you also love one another. By this all will know that you are My disciples, if you have love for one another.

JOHN 13:34-35

His Relationships

*L*ord, I pray that You would enable my husband to be a forgiving person and not carry grudges or hold things in his heart against others.

I pray that my husband would never be blinded by the darkness of unforgiveness, but continually walk in the light of forgiveness. Enable him to love his enemies, bless those who curse him, do good to those who hate him, and pray for those who spitefully use him and persecute him (Matthew 5:44).

I pray that I will be counted as his best friend and our friendship will continue to grow.

If you bring your gift to the altar, and there remember that your brother has something against you, leave your gift there before the altar, and go your way. First be reconciled to your brother, and then come and offer your gift.

MATTHEW 5:23-24

His Fatherhood

*L*ord, teach (husband's name) to be a good father. Where it was not modeled to him according to Your ways, heal those areas and help him to forgive his dad.

Give him revelation of You and a hunger in his heart to really know You as his heavenly Father. Draw him close to spend time in Your presence so he can become more like You and fully understand Your Father's heart of compassion and love toward him.

Grow that same heart in him for his children. Help him to balance mercy, judgment, and instruction the way You do. Though You require obedience, You are quick to acknowledge a repentant heart. Make him that way, too.

*Whom the L*ORD *loves He corrects, just as a father the son in whom he delights.*

PROVERBS 3:12

His Fatherhood

*L*ord, I pray that my husband will understand how to discipline our children properly. May he never provoke his children to wrath, but bring them up in the training and admonition of the Lord (Ephesians 6:4).

I pray we will be united in the rules we set for our children and be in full agreement as to how they are raised.

I pray that there will be no strife or argument over how to handle them and the issues that surround their lives. Give him skills of communication with his children.

I pray he will not be thought of by them as stern, hard, cruel, cold, and abusive, but rather may they see him as kind, softhearted, loving, warm, and affirming.

Children's children are the crown of old men, and the glory of children is their father.

PROVERBS 17:6

His Fatherhood

*L*ord, I pray that my husband will inspire his children to honor him as their father so that their lives will be long and blessed.

May he delight in his children and long to grow them up Your way. Help him not to be noncommunicative, passive, critical, weak, uninterested, neglectful, undependable, or uninvolved.

Make him, instead, the kind of father who is interested, affectionate, involved, strong, consistent, dependable, verbally communicative, understanding, and patient. Being a good father is something he wants very much. I pray that You would give him that desire of his heart.

The father of the righteous will greatly rejoice,
and he who begets a wise child will delight in him.

PROVERBS 23:24

His Past

*L*ord, I pray that You would enable (husband's name) to let go of his past completely. Deliver him from any hold it has on him. Help him to put off his former conduct and habitual ways of thinking about it and be renewed in his mind (Ephesians 4:22-23).

Enlarge his understanding to know that You make all things new (Revelation 21:5).

Show him a fresh, Holy Spirit-inspired way of relating to negative things that have happened. Give him the mind of Christ so that he can clearly discern Your voice from the voices of the past.

When he hears those old voices, enable him to rise up and shut them down with the truth of Your Word.

If anyone is in Christ, he is a new creation; old things have passed away; behold, all things have become new.

2 CORINTHIANS 5:17

His Past

*L*ord, I pray that wherever my husband has experienced rejection in his past, he would not allow that to color what he sees and hears now. May he regard the past as only a history lesson and not a guide for his daily life.

Wherever his past has become an unpleasant memory, I pray You would redeem it and bring life out of it. Bind up his wounds (Psalm 147:3). Restore his soul (Psalm 23:3).

Help him to release the past so that he will not live in it, but learn from it, break out of it, and move into the future You have for him.

Do not remember the former things, nor consider the things of old. Behold, I will do a new thing, now it shall spring forth; shall you not know it? I will even make a road in the wilderness and rivers in the desert.

ISAIAH 43:18-19

His Attitude

*L*ord, fill (husband's name) with Your love and peace today. May there be a calmness, serenity, and sense of well-being established in him because his life is God-controlled, rather than flesh-controlled. Enable him to walk in his house with a clean and perfect heart before You (Psalm 101:2).

Shine the light of Your Spirit upon him and fill him with Your love. I pray that he will be kind and patient, not selfish or easily provoked.

Enable him to bear all things, believe all things, hope all things, and endure all things (1 Corinthians 13:7).

Be anxious for nothing, but in everything by prayer and supplication, with thanksgiving, let your requests be made known to God; and the peace of God, which surpasses all understanding, will guard your hearts and minds through Christ Jesus.

PHILIPPIANS 4:6-7

His Attitude

*L*ord, I pray that my husband will have a heart of thanksgiving. May he not be broken in spirit because of sorrow (Proverbs 15:13), but enjoy the continual feast of a merry heart (Proverbs 15:15).

Help him to be anxious for nothing, but give thanks in all things so he can know the peace that passes all understanding. May he come to the point of saying, I have learned in whatever state I am, to be content (Philippians 4:11).

I say to (husband's name) this day, The Lord bless you and keep you; the Lord make His face shine upon you, and be gracious to you; the Lord lift up His countenance upon you, and give you peace (Numbers 6:24-26).

Enter into His gates with thanksgiving, and into His courts with praise. Be thankful to Him, and bless His name.

PSALM 100:4

His Marriage

*L*ord, I pray You would protect our marriage from anything that would harm or destroy it. Shield it from our own selfishness and neglect, from the evil plans and desires of others, and from unhealthy or dangerous situations.

May there be no thoughts of divorce or infidelity in our hearts, and none in our future. Set us free from past hurts, memories, and ties from previous relationships, and unrealistic expectations of one another.

Let nothing come into our hearts and habits that would threaten our marriage in any way.

Two are better than one, because they have a good reward for their labor. For if they fall, one will lift up his companion. But woe to him who is alone when he falls, for he has no one to help him up.

ECCLESIASTES 4:9-10

His Marriage

*L*ord, I pray that You would unite my husband and me in a bond of friendship, commitment, generosity, and understanding. Eliminate our immaturity, hostility, or feelings of inadequacy.

Help us to make time for one another alone, to nurture and renew our marriage and remind ourselves of the reasons we were married in the first place.

I pray that (husband's name) will be so committed to You, Lord, that his commitment to me will not waver, no matter what storms come.

I pray that our love for each other will grow stronger every day, so that we will never leave a legacy of divorce to our children.

Now to the married I command, yet not I but the Lord: A wife is not to depart from her husband. But even if she does depart, let her remain unmarried or be reconciled to her husband. And a husband is not to divorce his wife.

1 CORINTHIANS 7:10-11

His Emotions

*L*ord, You have said in Your Word that You redeem our souls when we put our trust in You (Psalm 34:22). I pray that (husband's name) would have faith in You to redeem his soul from negative emotions. May he never be controlled by depression, anger, anxiety, jealousy, hopelessness, fear, or suicidal thoughts.

I know that only You can deliver and heal, but use me as Your instrument of restoration. Help me not to be pulled down with him when he struggles. Enable me instead to understand and have words to say that will bring life.

I waited patiently for the LORD; and He inclined to me, and heard my cry. He also brought me up out of a horrible pit, out of the miry clay, and set my feet upon a rock, and established my steps. He has put a new song in my mouth—praise to our God; many will see it and fear, and will trust in the LORD.

PSALM 40:1-3

His Emotions

*L*ord, I pray that You would set my husband free of negative emotions. Release him to share his deepest feelings with me and others who can help.

Liberate him to cry when he needs to and not bottle his emotions inside. At the same time, give him the gift of laughter and ability to find humor in even serious situations.

Teach him to take his eyes off his circumstances and trust in You, regardless of how he is feeling. Give him patience to possess his soul and the ability to take charge of it (Luke 21:9).

Anoint him with the oil of joy (Isaiah 61:3), refresh him with Your Spirit, and set him free from any destructive emotions this day.

He who trusts in his own heart is a fool, but whoever walks wisely will be delivered.

PROVERBS 28:26

His Walk

O Lord, I know the way of man is not in himself; it is not in man who walks to direct his own steps (Jeremiah 10:23). Therefore, Lord, I pray that *You* would direct my husband's steps. Lead him in *Your* light, teach him *Your* way, so he will walk in *Your* truth.

I pray that he would have a deeper walk with You and an ever-progressing hunger for Your Word. May Your presence be like a delicacy he never ceases to crave.

Lead him on Your path and make him quick to confess when he strays from it. Reveal to him any hidden sin that would hinder him from walking rightly before You. May he experience deep repentance when he doesn't live in obedience to Your laws.

Lord, who may abide in Your tabernacle? Who may dwell in Your holy hill? He who walks uprightly, and works righteousness, and speaks the truth in his heart.

PSALM 15:1-2

His Walk

*L*ord, I pray that You would create a clean heart in my husband and renew a steadfast spirit within him. Don't cast him away from Your presence, and do not take Your Holy Spirit from him (Psalm 51:10-11).

I pray that You will enable (husband's name) to walk in the Spirit and not in the flesh and thereby keep himself from the paths of the destroyer (Psalm 17:4).

As he walks in the Spirit, may he bear the fruit of the Spirit, which is love, joy, peace, patience, kindness, goodness, faithfulness, gentleness, and self-control (Galatians 5:22-23).

He who walks righteously and speaks uprightly, he who despises the gain of oppressions, who gestures with his hands, refusing bribes, who stops his ears from hearing of bloodshed, and shuts his eyes from seeing evil: he will dwell on high; his place of defense will be the fortress of rocks; bread will be given him, his water will be sure.

ISAIAH 33:15-16

His Talk

*L*ord, I pray Your Holy Spirit would guard my husband's mouth so that he will speak only words that edify and bring life. Help him to not be a grumbler, complainer, a user of foul language, or one who destroys with his words, but be disciplined enough to keep his conversation godly.

Your Word says a man who desires a long life must keep his tongue from evil and his lips from speaking deceit (Psalm 34:12-13).

Show him how to do that. Fill him with Your love so that out of the overflow of his heart will come words that build up and not tear down. Work that in my heart as well.

Let no corrupt word proceed out of your mouth, but what is good for necessary edification, that it may impart grace to the hearers.

EPHESIANS 4:29

His Talk

$\mathscr{L}$ord, may Your Spirit of love reign in the words my husband and I speak to each other so that we don't miscommunicate or wound one another. Help us to show each other respect, speak words that encourage, share our feelings openly, and come to mutual agreements without strife.

Lord, You've said in Your Word that when two agree, You are in their midst. I pray that the reverse be true as well—that You will be in our midst so that we two can agree.

Let the words of our mouths and the meditations of our hearts be acceptable in Your sight, O Lord, our strength and our Redeemer (Psalm 19:14).

The words of a wise man's mouth are gracious,
but the lips of a fool shall swallow him up.

ECCLESIASTES 10:12

His Repentance

*L*ord, I pray that You would convict my husband of any error in his life. Let there be nothing covered that will not be revealed, and hidden that will not be known (Matthew 10:26).

Cleanse him from any secret sins and teach him to be a person who is quick to confess when he is wrong (Psalm 19:12).

Help him to recognize his mistakes. Bring him to full repentance before You. Lord, I know that humility must come before honor (Proverbs 15:33).

Take away all pride that would cause him to deny his faults and work into his soul a humility of heart so that he will receive the honor You have for him.

Search me, O God, and know my heart; try me, and know my anxieties; and see if there is any wicked way in me, and lead me in the way everlasting.

PSALM 139:23-24

His Deliverance

*L*ord, You have said to call upon You in the day of trouble and You will deliver us (Psalm 50:15). I call upon You now and ask that You would work deliverance in my husband's life. Deliver him from anything that binds him.

Bring him to a place of understanding where he can cry out to You for help. If the deliverance he prays for isn't immediate, keep him from discouragement and help him to be confident that You have begun a good work in him and will complete it (Philippians 1:6).

Give him the certainty that even in his most hopeless state, when he finds it impossible to change anything, You, Lord, can change everything.

~

The Lord is my rock and my fortress and my deliverer; my God, my strength, in whom I will trust; my shield and the horn of my salvation, my stronghold. I will call upon the Lord, who is worthy to be praised; so shall I be saved from my enemies.

PSALM 18:2-3

His Deliverance

*L*ord, help my husband to be strong in You so that he will be delivered from his enemy. Enable him to put on the whole armor of God, so he can stand against the wiles of the devil in the evil day. Help him to gird his waist with truth and put on the breastplate of righteousness, having shod his feet with the preparation of the gospel of peace. Enable him to take up the shield of faith, with which to quench all the fiery darts of the wicked one.

I pray that he will take the helmet of salvation, and the sword of the Spirit, which is the Word of God, praying always with all prayer and supplication in the Spirit, being watchful and standing strong to the end (Ephesians 6:13-18).

Because he has set his love upon Me, therefore I will deliver him; I will set him on high, because he has known My name.

PSALM 91:14

His Obedience

*L*ord, You have said in Your Word that if we regard iniquity in our hearts, You will not hear (Psalm 66:18). I want You to hear my prayers, so I ask You to reveal where there is any disobedience in my life, especially with regard to my husband.

Show me if I'm selfish, unloving, critical, angry, resentful, unforgiving, or bitter toward him. I confess it as sin and ask for Your forgiveness.

I pray that You would also give (husband's name) a desire to live in obedience to Your laws and Your ways. Reveal and uproot anything he willingly gives place to that is not of You. Help him to bring every thought and action under Your control.

My son, do not forget my law, but let your heart keep my commands; for length of days and long life and peace they will add to you. Let not mercy and truth forsake you; bind them around your neck, write them on the tablet of your heart.

PROVERBS 3:1-3

His Obedience

*L*ord, I pray that You would give my husband a heart to obey You. Reward him according to his righteousness and according to the cleanness of his hands (Psalm 18:20).

Show him Your ways, O Lord; teach him Your paths. Lead him in Your truth, for You are the God of his salvation (Psalm 25:4-5). Make him a praising person, for I know that when we worship You we gain clear understanding, our lives are transformed, and we receive power to live Your way.

Help him to hear Your specific instructions to him and enable him to obey them. Give him a longing to do Your will and may he enjoy the peace that can only come from living in total obedience to Your commands.

Obey My voice, and I will be your God, and you shall be My people. And walk in all the ways that I have commanded you, that it may be well with you.

JEREMIAH 7:23

His Self-Image

*L*ord, I pray that (husband's name) will find his identity in You. Help him to understand his worth through Your eyes and by Your standards. May he recognize the unique qualities You've placed in him and be able to appreciate them.

Enable him to see himself the way You see him, understanding that You have made him a little lower than the angels, and You have crowned him with glory and honor.

Quiet the voices that tell him otherwise and give him ears to hear Your voice telling him that it will not be his perfection that gets him through life successfully—it will be Yours.

We all, with unveiled face, beholding as in a mirror the glory of the Lord, are being transformed into the same image from glory to glory, just as by the Spirit of the Lord.

2 CORINTHIANS 3:18

His Self-Image

*L*ord, I pray that You would reveal to my husband that he is the image and glory of God (1 Corinthians 11:7), and he is complete in Him, who is the head of all principality and power (Colossians 2:10).

Give him the peace and security of knowing that he is accepted, not rejected, by You. Free him from the self-focus and self-consciousness that can imprison his soul.

Help him to see who *You* really are so he'll know who *he* really is. May his true self-image be the image of Christ stamped upon his soul.

I say to you, (husband's name), Arise, shine; for your light has come! And the glory of the Lord is risen upon you (Isaiah 60:1).

Whom He foreknew, He also predestined to be conformed to the image of His Son, that He might be the firstborn among many brethren.

ROMANS 8:29

His Faith

*L*ord, I pray that You will give (husband's name) an added measure of faith today. Enlarge his ability to believe in You, Your Word, Your promises, Your ways, and Your power. Put a longing in his heart to talk with You and hear Your voice.

Give him an understanding of what it means to bask in Your presence and not just ask for things. May he seek You, rely totally upon You, be led by You, put You first, and acknowledge You in everything he does. Lord, You have said in Your Word that whatever is not from faith is sin (Romans 14:23).

May my husband be free from the sin of doubt in his life.

Let him ask in faith, with no doubting, for he who doubts is like a wave of the sea driven and tossed by the wind. For let not that man suppose that he will receive anything from the Lord; he is a double-minded man, unstable in all his ways.

JAMES 1:6-8

His Faith

*L*ord, You've said that faith comes by hearing, and hearing by the word of God (Romans 10:17). I pray that You would feed my husband's soul with Your Word so his faith grows big enough to believe that with You all things are possible (Matthew 19:26).

Give him unfailing certainty that what You've promised to do, You will do (Romans 4:21). Make his faith a shield of protection. Put it into action to move the mountains in his life. Your Word says, The just shall live by faith (Romans 1:17); I pray that he will live the kind of faith-filled life You've called us all to experience.

May he know with complete certainty how great is Your goodness, which You have laid up for those who fear You, which You have prepared for those who trust in You (Psalm 31:19).

Having been justified by faith, we have peace with God through our Lord Jesus Christ.

ROMANS 5:1

His Future

*L*ord, I pray that You would give (husband's name) a vision for his future. Help him to understand that Your plans for him are good and not evil—to give him a future and a hope (Jeremiah 29:11).

Fill him with the knowledge of Your will in all wisdom and spiritual understanding that he may have a walk worthy of You, fully pleasing You, being fruitful in every good work and increasing in the knowledge of You (Colossians 1:9-10).

May he live by the leading of the Holy Spirit and not walk in doubt and fear of what may happen. Help him to mature and grow in You daily, submitting to You all his dreams and desires, knowing that the things which are impossible with men are possible with God (Luke 18:27).

*I know the thoughts that I think toward you, says the L*ORD*, thoughts of peace and not of evil, to give you a future and a hope.*

JEREMIAH 29:11

His Future

～∽∽～

*L*ord, I pray that (husband's name) will always conduct himself in a way that invests in his future. Keep him from losing his sense of purpose and fill him with hope for his future as an anchor of the soul, both sure and steadfast (Hebrews 6:19).

Give him his heart's desire (Psalm 21:2) and keep him fresh and flourishing and bearing fruit into old age (Psalm 92:13-14).

And when it comes time for him to leave this earth and go to be with You, may he have such a strong vision for his eternal future that it makes his transition smooth, painless, and accompanied by peace and joy. Until that day, I pray he will find the vision for his future in You.

～∽～

One thing I have desired of the LORD, that will I seek: that I may dwell in the house of the LORD all the days of my life, to behold the beauty of the LORD, and to inquire in His temple.

PSALM 27:4

PART V

The Power
of a
PRAYING
PARENT

Becoming a
Praying Parent

*L*ord, I submit myself to You. I realize that parenting a child in the way You would have me to is beyond my human abilities. I know I need You to help me. I want to partner with You and partake of Your gifts of wisdom, discernment, revelation, and guidance. I also need Your strength and patience, along with a generous portion of Your love flowing through me.

Teach me how to love the way You love. Where I need to be healed, delivered, changed, matured, or made whole, I invite You to do that in me. Help me to walk in righteousness and integrity before You.

Teach me Your ways, enable me to obey Your commandments and do only what is pleasing in Your sight.

The righteous man walks in his integrity; his children are blessed after him.

PROVERBS 20:7

Becoming a Praying Parent

*L*ord, may the beauty of Your Spirit be so evident in me that I will be a godly role model for my child. Give me the communication, teaching, and nurturing skills that I must have.

Grow me into being the kind of parent You want me to be and teach me how to pray and truly intercede for his (her) life. You said in Your Word, Whatever things you ask in prayer, believing, you will receive (Matthew 21:22).

In Jesus' name I ask that You will increase my faith to believe for all the things You have put on my heart to pray for concerning this child.

Whatever you ask in My name, that I will do, that the Father may be glorified in the Son. If you ask anything in My name, I will do it.

JOHN 14:13-14

Releasing My Child
into God's Hands

*L*ord, I come to You in Jesus' name and give (name of child) to You. I'm convinced that You alone know what is best for him (her).

You alone know what he (she) needs. I release him (her) to You to care for and protect, and I commit myself to pray for everything concerning him (her) that I can think of or that You put upon my heart.

Teach me how to pray and guide me in what to pray about. Help me not to impose my own will when I'm praying for him (her), but rather enable me to pray that Your will be done in his (her) life. Thank You that I can partner with You in raising him (her) and that I don't have to do it alone.

The mercy of the LORD is from everlasting to ever-lasting on those who fear Him, and His righteousness to children's children, to such as keep His covenant, and to those who remember His commandments to do them.

PSALM 103:17-18

Releasing My Child into God's Hands

Thank You, Lord, for the precious gift of this child. Because Your Word says that every good gift comes from You, I know that You have given him (her) to me to care for and raise.

Help me to do that. Show me places where I continue to hang on to him (her) and enable me to release him (her) to Your protection, guidance, and counsel.

Help me not to live in fear of possible dangers, but in the joy and peace of knowing that You are in control. I'm grateful that I don't have to rely on the world's unreliable and everchanging methods of child rearing, but that I can have clear directions from Your Word and wisdom as I pray to You for answers. I rely on You for everything, and this day I trust my child to You and release him (her) into Your hands.

If you then, being evil, know how to give good gifts to your children, how much more will your Father who is in heaven give good things to those who ask Him!

MATTHEW 7:11

Releasing My Child into God's Hands

*L*ord, I am raising my children in (name of city). I invite You to reign in this community. Pour out Your Spirit upon everyone so that all people will be drawn to You. Make our streets safe from accidents and evil people. Take evil people with evil intentions toward our children out of this city and out of our lives. Bless and protect my children and all the children of our city. Remind me to pray for my city often, and show me how I can join in prayer with others so that it can be a wonderful place to raise children.

Far be it from me that I should sin against the Lord in ceasing to pray for you.

1 SAMUEL 12:23

Securing Protection from Harm

*L*ord, I lift (name of child) up to You and ask that You would put a hedge of protection around her (him). Protect her (his) spirit, body, mind, and emotions from any kind of evil or harm.

I pray specifically for protection from accidents, disease, injury, or any other physical, mental, or emotional abuse.

I pray that she (he) will make her (his) refuge in the shadow of Your wings until these calamities have passed by (Psalm 57:1).

Hide her (him) from any kind of evil influences that would come against her (him).

When you pass through the waters, I will be with you; and through the rivers, they shall not overflow you. When you walk through the fire, you shall not be burned, nor shall the flame scorch you.

ISAIAH 43:2

Securing Protection from Harm

Thank You, Lord, for Your many promises of protection. I pray that You will put a hedge of safety and protection around (name of child) on every side and keep her (him) away from harm.

Protect her (him) from any hidden dangers and let no weapon formed against her (him) be able to prosper.

Help her (him) to walk in Your ways and in obedience to Your will so that she (he) never comes out from under the umbrella of that protection.

Keep her (him) safe in all she (he) does and wherever she (he) goes. In Jesus' name, I pray.

Because you have made the LORD, who is my refuge, even the Most High, your dwelling place, no evil shall befall you, nor shall any plague come near your dwelling.

PSALM 91:9-10

Feeling Loved and Accepted

*L*ord, I pray for (name of child) to feel loved and accepted. Penetrate his (her) heart with Your love right now and help him (her) to fully understand how far-reaching and complete it is. Your Word says You loved us so much that You sent Your Son to die for us (John 3:16).

Deliver him (her) from any lies of the enemy that may have been planted in his (her) mind to cause him (her) to doubt that. Lord, help (name of child) to abide in Your love. May he (she) say as David did, Cause me to hear Your lovingkindness in the morning, for in You do I trust (Psalm 143:8).

Manifest Your love to this child in a real way today and help him (her) to receive it.

God is love, and he who abides in love abides in God, and God in him.

1 JOHN 4:16

Feeling Loved and Accepted

*L*ord, I pray that You would help me to love this child unconditionally the way You do, and enable me to show it in a manner he (she) can perceive.

Reveal to me how I can demonstrate and model Your love to him (her) so that it will be clearly understood. I pray that all my family members will love and accept him (her), and may he (she) find favor with other people as well.

With each day that he (she) grows in the confidence of being loved and accepted, as he (she) comes to fully understand the depth of Your love for him (her), make him (her) a vessel through which Your love flows to others.

In this is love, not that we loved God, but that He loved us and sent His Son to be the propitiation for our sins. Beloved, if God so loved us, we also ought to love one another.

1 JOHN 4:10-11

Establishing an Eternal Future

Lord, I bring (name of child) before You and ask that You would help her (him) grow into a deep understanding of who You are.

Open her (his) heart and bring her (him) to a full knowledge of the truth about You. Lord, You have said in Your Word, If you confess with your mouth the Lord Jesus and believe in your heart that God has raised Him from the dead, you will be saved (Romans 10:9).

I pray for that kind of faith for my child. May she (he) call You her (his) Savior, be filled with Your Holy Spirit, acknowledge You in every area of her (his) life, and choose always to follow You and Your ways. Help her (him) to fully believe that Jesus laid down His life for her (him) so that she (he) might have life eternally and abundantly now.

This is the will of Him who sent Me, that everyone who sees the Son and believes in Him may have everlasting life; and I will raise him up at the last day.

JOHN 6:40

Establishing an Eternal Future

*L*ord, I pray that (name of child) will live a fruitful life, ever increasing in the knowledge of You. May she (he) always know Your will, have spiritual understanding, and walk in a manner that is pleasing in Your sight. You have said in Your Word that You will pour out Your Spirit on my offspring (Isaiah 44:3).

Thank You, Lord, that You care about her (his) eternal future even more than I do and that it is secure in You.

In Jesus' name I pray that she (he) will not doubt or stray from the path You have for her (him) all the days of her (his) life.

I will pray the Father, and He will give you another Helper, that He may abide with you forever—the Spirit of truth, whom the world cannot receive, because it neither sees Him nor knows Him; but you know Him, for He dwells with you and will be in you.

JOHN 14:16-17

Honoring Parents and Resisting Rebellion

⋘∘⋙

*L*ord, I pray that You would give (name of child) a heart that desires to obey You. Put into him (her) a longing to spend time with You, in Your Word and in prayer, listening for Your voice. Shine Your light upon any secret or unseen rebellion that is taking root in his (her) heart, so that it can be identified and destroyed.

Lord, I pray that he (she) will not give himself (herself) over to pride, selfishness, and rebellion, but that he (she) will be delivered from it. By the authority You've given me in Jesus' name, I stand against the wiles of the devil and I resist idolatry, rebellion, stubbornness, and disrespect; they will have no part in my son's (daughter's) life, nor will my child walk a path of destruction and death because of them.

⋘∘⋙

The eye that mocks his father, and scorns obedience to his mother, the ravens of the valley will pick it out, and the young eagles will eat it.

PROVERBS 30:17

Honoring Parents
and Resisting Rebellion

$\mathcal{L}$ord, Your Word instructs, Children, obey your parents in all things, for this is well pleasing to the Lord (Colossians 3:20).

I pray that You would turn the heart of (name of child) toward his (her) parents and enable him (her) to honor and obey both father and mother so that his (her) life will be long and good. Turn his (her) heart toward You so that all he (she) does is pleasing in Your sight.

Help him (her) to know the beauty and simplicity of walking with a sweet and humble spirit in obedience and submission to You.

My son, hear the instruction of your father, and do not forsake the law of your mother; for they will be a graceful ornament on your head, and chains about your neck.

PROVERBS 1:8-9

Maintaining Good
Family Relationships

*L*ord, I pray for (name of child) and her (his) relationship with all family members. Protect and preserve them from any unresolved or permanent breach.

Fill her (his) heart with Your love and give her (him) an abundance of compassion and forgiveness that will overflow to each member of the family.

Specifically, I pray for a close, happy, loving, and fulfilling relationship between (name of child) and (name of family member) for all the days of their lives. May there always be good communication between them and may unforgiveness have no root in their hearts.

Help them to love, value, appreciate, and respect one another so that the God-ordained tie between them cannot be broken.

Blessed are the peacemakers, for they shall be called sons of God.

MATTHEW 5:9

Maintaining Good
Family Relationships

❧❧❧

*L*ord, I pray that You would teach my child to resolve misunderstandings according to Your Word. And if any division has already begun, if any relationship is strained or severed, Lord, I pray that You will drive out the wedge of division and bring healing. I pray that there be no strain, breach, misunderstanding, arguing, fighting, or separating of ties. Your Word instructs us to be of one mind, having compassion for one another; love as brothers, be tenderhearted, be courteous (1 Peter 3:8). Help her (him) to live accordingly, endeavoring to keep the unity of the Spirit in the bond of peace (Ephesians 4:3). In Jesus' name I pray that You would instill a love and compassion in her (him) for all family members that is strong and unending, like a cord that cannot be broken.

❧

Behold, how good and how pleasant it is for brethren to dwell together in unity!

PSALM 133:1

Attracting Godly Friends and Role Models

※※※

*L*ord, I lift up (name of child) to You and ask that You would bring godly friends and role models into his (her) life. Give him (her) the wisdom he (she) needs to choose friends who are godly and help him (her) to never compromise his (her) walk with You in order to gain acceptance. I pray that You would take anyone who is not a godly influence out of his (her) life or else transform that person into Your likeness. Your Word says, He who walks with wise men will be wise, but the companion of fools will be destroyed (Proverbs 13:20). Enable him (her) to walk with wise friends and not have to experience the destruction that can happen by walking with foolish people.

※※

Make no friendship with an angry man, and with a furious man do not go, lest you learn his ways and set a snare for your soul.

PROVERBS 22:24-25

Attracting Godly Friends and Role Models

❧⟡❧

*L*ord, I pray that You would deliver (name of child) from anyone in her life who has an ungodly character so that he (she) will not learn that person's ways and set a snare for his (her) own soul.

Whenever there is grief over a lost friendship, comfort him (her) and send new friends with whom he (she) can connect, share, and be the person You created him (her) to be.

Lord, please take away any loneliness or low self-esteem that would cause him (her) to seek out less than God-glorifying relationships. In Jesus' name I pray that You would teach him (her) the meaning of true friendship.

Teach him (her) how to be a good friend and make strong, close, lasting relationships. May each of his (her) friendships always glorify You.

❧⟡❧

Do not enter the path of the wicked, and do not walk in the way of evil.

PROVERBS 4:14

Developing a Hunger for the Things of God

Lord, I pray for (name of child) to have an ever-increasing hunger for more of You. May she (he) long for Your presence—long to spend time with You in prayer, praise, and worship. Give her (him) a desire for the truth of Your Word and a love for Your laws and Your ways. Teach her (him) to live by faith and be led by the Holy Spirit, having an availability to do what You tell her (him) to do. May she (he) not have any allegiances or diversions away from You, but rather may she (he) be repulsed by ungodliness and all that is in opposition to You. May a deep reverence and love for You and Your ways color everything she (he) does and every choice she (he) makes. May she (he) not be wise in her (his) own eyes, but rather fear the Lord and depart from evil (Proverbs 3:7).

Blessed are those who hunger and thirst for righteousness, for they shall be filled.

MATTHEW 5:6

Developing a Hunger for the Things of God

❧❧❧

*L*ord, I pray that (name of child) will develop a deep hunger for You. Help him (her) to love You so much that praising and worshiping You becomes a way of life. I pray that he (she) will have a desire for Your holiness to permeate his (her) entire being so that he (she) lives a life set apart for Your purposes. Help him (her) to be focused on You all the days of his (her) life.

❧❧

*Worship the L*ord *in the beauty of holiness.*

PSALM 29:2

Developing a Hunger for the Things of God

~~~~~

*L*ord, I pray that You will help (name of child) to be reliable, dependable, responsible, compassionate, sensitive, loving, and giving to others. Deliver her (him) from any pride, laziness, slothfulness, selfishness, or lust of the flesh. I pray that she (he) will have a teachable and submissive spirit, yet be able to stand strong in her (his) convictions. I pray that she (he) will always desire to belong to a Christian church that is alive to the truth of Your Word and the power of Holy Spirit-led worship and prayer. Write Your law in her (his) mind and on her (his) heart so that she (he) always walks with a confident assurance of the righteousness of Your commands. As she (he) learns to pray, teach her (him) to listen for Your voice. May there always be a Holy Spirit fire in her (his) heart and an unwavering desire for the things of God.

~~~~~

Blessed are those who keep His testimonies, who seek Him with the whole heart!

PSALM 119:2

Being the Person God Created

*L*ord, I pray that You would pour out Your Spirit upon (name of child) this day and anoint him (her) for all that You've called him (her) to be and do. May he (she) never stray from Your path and try to be something he (she) was not created to be.

Deliver him (her) from any evil plan of the devil to rob him (her) of life, to steal away his (her) uniqueness and giftedness, to compromise the path You've called him (her) to walk, or to destroy the person You created him (her) to be.

May he (she) not be a follower of anyone but You, but may he (she) be a leader of people into Your kingdom. May the fruit of the Spirit, which is love, joy, peace, patience, kindness, goodness, faithfulness, gentleness, and self-control, grow in him (her) daily (Galatians 5:22).

Be even more diligent to make your call and election sure, for if you do these things you will never stumble.

2 PETER 1:10

Being the Person God Created

Lord, I pray that (name of child) will find his (her) identity in You. Help him (her) to view himself (herself) as Your instrument and know without doubt that in You he (she) is complete. Give him (her) a vision for his (her) life when setting goals for the future and a sense of purpose about what You've called him (her) to do. Help him (her) to see himself (herself) as You do—from his (her) future and not from his (her) past. Teach him (her) to look to You as his (her) hope for the future.

May his (her) commitment to being who You created him (her) to be enable him (her) to grow daily in confidence and Holy Spirit boldness.

Eye has not seen, nor ear heard, nor have entered into the heart of man the things which God has prepared for those who love Him.

1 CORINTHIANS 2:9

Following Truth, Rejecting Lies

*L*ord, I pray that You will fill (name of child) with Your Spirit of truth. Give her (him) a heart that loves truth and follows after it, rejecting all lies as a manifestation of the enemy.

Flush out anything in her (him) that would entertain a lying spirit and cleanse her (him) from any death that has crept in as a result of lies she (he) may have spoken or thought.

I pray that she (he) not be blinded or deceived, but always be able to clearly understand Your truth.

Let not mercy and truth forsake you; bind them around your neck, write them on the tablet of your heart, and so find favor and high esteem in the sight of God and man.

PROVERBS 3:3-4

Following Truth, Rejecting Lies

❦

*L*ord, I pray that (name of child) will never be able to get away with lying—that all lies will come to light and be exposed. If she (he) lies, may she (he) be so miserable that confession and its consequences will seem like a relief.

Help me to teach her (him) what it means to lie, and effectively discipline her (him) when she (he) tests that principle. Your Word says that when He, the Spirit of truth, has come, He will guide you into all truth (John 16:13).

❦

If you love Me, keep My commandments. And I will pray the Father, and He will give you another Helper, that He may abide with you forever—the Spirit of truth, whom the world cannot receive, because it neither sees Him nor knows Him; but you know Him, for He dwells with you and will be in you.

JOHN 14:15-17

Enjoying a Life of Health and Healing

*L*ord, because You have instructed us in Your Word that we are to pray for one another so that we may be healed, I pray for healing and wholeness for (name of child). I pray that sickness and infirmity will have no place or power in his (her) life.

I pray for protection against any disease coming into his (her) body. Your Word says, He sent His word and healed them, and delivered them from their destructions (Psalm 107:20).

Wherever there is disease, illness, or infirmity in his (her) body, I pray that You, Lord, would touch him (her) with Your healing power and restore him (her) to total health.

Confess your trespasses to one another, and pray for one another, that you may be healed. The effective, fervent prayer of a righteous man avails much.

JAMES 5:16

Enjoying a Life of Health and Healing

❧⟋⟋❧

*L*ord, I pray that You would deliver (name of child) from any destruction, disease, or injury that could come upon him (her).

Specifically I ask You to heal (name any specific problem). When and if we are to see a doctor, I pray that You, Lord, would show us who that should be. Give that doctor wisdom and full knowledge of the best way to proceed.

Thank You, Lord, that You suffered and died for us so that we might be healed. I lay claim to that heritage of healing which You have promised in Your Word and provided for those who believe. I look to You for a life of health, healing, and wholeness for my child.

❧⟋❧

But to you who fear My name the Sun of Righteousness shall arise with healing in His wings.

MALACHI 4:2

Having the Motivation for Proper Body Care

*L*ord, I lift (name of child) to You and ask that You would place in her (him) the desire to eat healthy food. Help her (him) to understand what's good for her (him) and what isn't, and give her (him) a desire for food that is healthful.

I pray that she (he) be spared from all eating disorders in any form. Along with the desire to eat properly, give her (him) the motivation to exercise regularly, to drink plenty of pure water, and to control and manage stress in her (his) life by living according to Your Word. Lord, Your Word says, You shall know the truth, and the truth shall make you free (John 8:32).

Help her (him) to see the truth about the way she (he) is to live, so that she (he) can be set free from any unhealthful habits.

Therefore, whether you eat or drink, or whatever you do, do all for the glory of God.

1 CORINTHIANS 10:31

Having the Motivation
for Proper Body Care

*L*ord, I pray that You would give (name of child) a vision of her (his) body as the temple of the Holy Spirit. I pray that she (he) will value the body You've given her (him) and desire to take proper care of it. May she (he) not be critical of it, nor examine herself (himself) through the microscope of public opinion and acceptance.

I pray that she (he) will not be bound by the lure of fashion magazines, television, or movies which try to influence her (him) with an image of what they say she (he) should look like. Help her (him) to see that what makes a person truly attractive is Your Holy Spirit living in her (him) and radiating outward. May she (he) come to understand that true attractiveness begins in the heart of one who loves God.

I beseech you therefore, brethren, by the mercies of God, that you present your bodies a living sacrifice, holy, acceptable to God, which is your reasonable service.

ROMANS 12:1

Instilling the Desire to Learn

❧

*L*ord, I pray that (name of child) will have a deep reverence for You and Your ways. May he (she) hide Your Word in his (her) heart like a treasure, and seek after understanding like silver or gold. Give him (her) a good mind, a teachable spirit, and an ability to learn. Instill in him (her) a desire to attain knowledge and skill, and may he (she) have joy in the process.

Above all, I pray that he (she) will be taught by You, for Your Word says that when our children are taught by You they are guaranteed peace.

You have also said, The fear of the LORD is the beginning of knowledge, but fools despise wisdom and instruction (Proverbs 1:7). May he (she) never be a fool and turn away from learning, but rather may he (she) turn to You for the knowledge he (she) needs.

❧

All your children shall be taught by the LORD, and great shall be the peace of your children.

ISAIAH 54:13

Instilling the Desire to Learn

❧

*L*ord, I pray that (name of child) will respect the wisdom of his (her) parents and be willing to be taught by them. Bring the perfect teachers into his (her) life who are godly people from whom he (she) can easily learn. Let him (her) find favor with his (her) teachers and have good communication with them.

Help him (her) to excel in school and do well in any classes he (she) may take. Make the pathways of learning smooth and not something with which he (she) must strain and struggle.

Give him (her) clarity of thought, organization, good memory, and strong learning ability. I say to him (her) according to Your Word, May the Lord give you understanding in all things (2 Timothy 2:7).

❧

Take firm hold of instruction, do not let go; keep her, for she is your life.

PROVERBS 4:13

Identifying God-Given Gifts and Talents

❧❦❧

*L*ord, I thank You for the gifts and talents You have placed in (name of child). I pray that You would develop them in her (him) and use them for Your glory. Your Word says, Having then gifts differing according to the grace that is given to us, let us use them (Romans 12:6). As she (he) recognizes the talents and abilities You've given her (him), I pray that no feelings of inadequacy, fear, or uncertainty will keep her (him) from using them according to Your will. May she (he) hear the call You have on her (his) life so that she (he) doesn't spend a lifetime trying to figure out what it is or miss it altogether.

❧❦❧

Every good gift and every perfect gift is from above, and comes down from the Father of lights, with whom there is no variation or shadow of turning.

JAMES 1:17

Identifying God-Given Gifts and Talents

❧

*L*ord, I pray You would reveal to (name of child) what her (his) life work is to be and help her (him) excel in it.

Bless the work of her (his) hands, and may she (he) be able to earn a good living doing the work she (he) loves and does best. Let her (his) talent never be wasted, watered down by mediocrity, or used to glorify anything or anyone other than You, Lord.

May whatever she (he) does find favor with others and be well received and respected. But most of all, I pray the gifts and talents You placed in her (him) be released to find their fullest expression in glorifying You.

❧

I thank my God always concerning you for the grace of God which was given to you by Christ Jesus, that you were enriched in every thing by Him in all utterance and all knowledge, even as the testimony of Christ was confirmed in you, so that you come short in no gift, eagerly waiting for the revelation of our Lord Jesus Christ.

1 CORINTHIANS 1:4-7

Learning to Speak Life

*L*ord, I pray that (name of child) will choose to use speech that glorifies You. Fill his (her) heart with Your Spirit and Your truth so that what overflows from his (her) mouth will be words of life and not death.

I pray that obscene or foul language be so foreign to him (her) that if words like that ever do find their way through his (her) lips, they will be like gravel in his (her) mouth and he (she) will be repulsed by them.

Help him (her) to hear himself (herself) so that words don't come out carelessly or thoughtlessly. I pray that by his (her) words he (she) will be justified (Matthew 12:37).

A good man out of the good treasure of his heart brings forth good things, and an evil man out of the evil treasure brings forth evil things.

MATTHEW 12:35

Learning to Speak Life

*L*ord, I pray that You would keep (name of child) from being snared by the words of his (her) mouth. You've promised that whoever guards his mouth and tongue keeps his soul from troubles (Proverbs 21:23). Help him (her) to put a guard over his (her) mouth and keep far away from adversity.

Your Word says that death and life are in the power of the tongue, and those who love it will eat its fruit (Proverbs 18:21). May he (she) speak life and not death. May he (she) be quick to listen and slow to speak so that his (her) speech will always be seasoned with grace. Equip him (her) to know how, what, and when to speak to anyone in any situation.

Let the words of my mouth and the meditation of my heart be acceptable in Your sight, O Lord, my strength and my Redeemer.

PSALM 19:14

Staying Attracted
to Holiness and Purity

*L*ord, I pray that You would fill (name of child) with a love for You that surpasses her (his) love for anything or anyone else. Help her (him) to respect and revere Your laws and understand that they are there for her (his) benefit.

Hide Your Word in her (his) heart so that there is no attraction to sin. I pray she (he) will run from evil, from impurity, from unholy thoughts, words, and deeds.

May she (he) be drawn toward whatever is pure and holy. Let Christ be formed in her (him) and cause her (him) to seek the power of Your Holy Spirit to enable her (him) to do what is right.

In a great house there are not only vessels of gold and silver, but also of wood and clay, some for honor and some for dishonor. Therefore if anyone cleanses himself from the latter, he will be a vessel of honor, sanctified and useful for the Master, prepared for every good work.

2 TIMOTHY 2:20-21

Staying Attracted to Holiness and Purity

~~~

*L*ord, You have said, Blessed are the pure in heart, for they shall see God (Matthew 5:8). May a desire for holiness that comes from a pure heart be reflected in all that she (he) does.

I pray that the clothes she (he) wears and the way she (he) styles her (his) hair and chooses to adorn her (his) body and face will reflect a reverence and a desire to glorify You, Lord.

Give her (him) understanding that to live in purity brings wholeness and blessing into her (his) life, and that the greatest reward for it is seeing You.

~~~

Who may ascend into the hill of the LORD? Or who may stand in His holy place? He who has clean hands and a pure heart, who has not lifted up his soul to an idol, nor sworn deceitfully. He shall receive blessing from the LORD, and righteousness from the God of his salvation.

PSALM 24:3-5

Praying Through
a Child's Room

❦

*L*ord, I invite Your Holy Spirit to dwell in the room that belongs to (name of child). You are Lord over heaven and earth, and I proclaim that You are Lord over this room as well. Flood it with Your light and life.

Crowd out any darkness which seeks to impose itself here, and let no spirits of fear, depression, anger, doubt, anxiety, rebelliousness, or hatred (name anything you've seen manifested in your child's behavior) find any place here.

I pray that nothing will come into his (her) room that is not brought by You, Lord. If there is anything here that shouldn't be, show me so it can be taken out. Give my child discernment about all that You find unacceptable.

❧

Nor shall you bring an abomination into your house, lest you be doomed to destruction like it.

DEUTERONOMY 7:26

Praying Through
a Child's Room

~~~

Lord, I pray that You would put Your complete protection over this room that belongs to (name of child) so that evil cannot enter here by any means. Fill his (her) room with Your love, peace, and joy. I pray that he (she) will say, as David did, I will walk within my house with a perfect heart. I will set nothing wicked before my eyes (Psalm 101:2-3).

I pray that You, Lord, will make this room a holy place, sanctified for Your glory. Cause him (her) to always want to cleanse himself from all filthiness of the flesh and spirit, perfecting holiness in the fear of God (2 Corinthians 7:1).

Lord, You have said that The curse of the Lord is on the house of the wicked, but He blesses the home of the just (Proverbs 3:33). Bless the habitation of this child.

~~~

Wash yourselves, make yourselves clean; put away the evil of your doings from before My eyes. Cease to do evil.

ISAIAH 1:16

Enjoying Freedom
from Fear

*L*ord, Your Word says, I sought the LORD, and He heard me, and delivered me from all my fears (Psalm 34:4). I seek You this day, believing that You hear me, and I pray that You will deliver (name of child) from any fear that threatens to overtake her (him). You said You have not given us a spirit of fear, but of power and of love and of a sound mind (2 Timothy 1:7).

Flood her (him) with Your love and wash away all fear and doubt. Give her (him) a sense of Your loving presence that far outweighs any fear that would threaten to overtake her (him).

Help her (him) to rely on Your power in such a manner that it establishes strong confidence and faith in You.

Fear not, for I am with you; be not dismayed, for I am your God. I will strengthen you, yes, I will help you, I will uphold you with My righteous right hand.

ISAIAH 41:10

Enjoying Freedom from Fear

*L*ord, You have said that There is no fear in love; but perfect love casts out fear, because fear involves torment (1 John 4:18). I pray that Your perfect love will surround (name of child) and give her (him) peace. Wherever there is real danger or good reason to fear, give her (him) wisdom, protect her (him) and draw her (him) close to You. Help her (him) not to deny her (his) fears, but take them to You in prayer and seek deliverance from them.

I pray that as she (he) draws close to You, Your love will penetrate her (his) life and crowd out all fear. Plant Your Word in her (his) heart. Let faith take root in her (his) mind and soul as she (he) grows in Your Word. Thank You, Lord, for Your promise to deliver us from all our fears. In Jesus' name I pray for freedom from fear on behalf of my child this day.

The LORD is the strength of my life; of whom shall I be afraid?

PSALM 27:1

Receiving
a Sound Mind

❧

*L*ord, thank You for promising us a sound mind. I lay claim to that promise for (name of child). I pray that his (her) mind be clear, alert, bright, intelligent, stable, peaceful, and uncluttered. I pray there will be no confusion, no dullness, and no unbalanced, scattered, unorganized, or negative thinking.

I pray that his (her) mind will not be filled with complex or confusing thoughts. Rather, give him (her) clarity of mind so that he (she) is able to think straight at all times.

Give him (her) the ability to make clear decisions, to understand all he (she) needs to know, and to be able to focus on what he (she) needs to do. Where there is now any mental instability, I speak healing in Jesus' name.

❧

God has not given us a spirit of fear, but of power and of love and of a sound mind.

2 TIMOTHY 1:7

Receiving
a Sound Mind

❧

*L*ord, I pray that (name of child) will so love You with all his (her) heart, soul, and mind that there will be no room in him (her) for the lies of the enemy or the clamoring of the world.

May the Word of God take root in his (her) heart and fill his (her) mind with things that are true, noble, just, pure, lovely, of good report, virtuous, and praiseworthy (Philippians 4:8).

Give him (her) understanding that what goes into his (her) mind becomes part of him (her), so that he (she) will weigh carefully what he (she) sees and hears.

I pray that his (her) faith in You and Your Word will grow daily so that he (she) will live forever in peace and soundness of mind.

❧

For to be carnally minded is death, but to be spiritually minded is life and peace.

ROMANS 8:6

Inviting the Joy
of the Lord

❦

*L*ord, I pray that (name of child) be given the gift of joy. Let the spirit of joy rise up in her (his) heart this day and may she (he) know the fullness of joy that is found only in Your presence. Help her (him) to understand that true happiness and joy are found only in You.

Whenever she (he) is overtaken by negative emotions, surround her (him) with Your love. Teach her (him) to say, This is the day that the LORD has made, [I] will rejoice and be glad in it (Psalm 118:24).

Deliver her (him) from despair, depression, loneliness, discouragement, anger, or rejection. May these negative attitudes have no place in (name of child), nor be a lasting part of her (his) life.

❦

If you keep My commandments, you will abide in My love, just as I have kept My Father's commandments and abide in His love. These things I have spoken to you, that My joy may remain in you, and that your joy may be full.

JOHN 15:10-11

Inviting the Joy
of the Lord

෬෬෬

*L*ord, I pray that You would plant Your Word firmly in (name of child). Etch it permanently on her (his) heart and increase her (his) faith daily. I know, Lord, that any negative emotions this child feels are lies, contrary to the truth of Your Word.

You have made her (him) to delight in You and not be anxious about anything. May she (he) decide in her (his) heart, My soul shall be joyful in the LORD; it shall rejoice in His salvation (Psalm 35:9).

I pray that You, the God of hope, will fill her (him) with joy and peace so that she (he) may abound in hope by the power of the Holy Spirit (Romans 15:13). Enable her (him) to abide in Your love and derive strength from the joy of knowing You this day and forever.

෬෬

You will show me the path of life; in Your presence is fullness of joy; at Your right hand are pleasures forevermore.

PSALM 16:11

Destroying an Inheritance
of Family Bondage

֍

*L*ord, You have said in Your Word that a good man leaves an inheritance to his children's children (Proverbs 13:22). I pray that the inheritance I leave to my children will be the rewards of a godly life and a clean heart before You. To make sure that happens, I ask that wherever there is any kind of bondage in me that I have inherited from my family and accepted as mine, deliver me from it now in the name of Jesus. I confess the sins of my family to You. I don't even know what all of them are, but I know that You do. I ask for forgiveness and restoration. I also confess my own sins to You and ask for forgiveness, knowing Your Word says, If we confess our sins, He is faithful and just to forgive us our sins and cleanse us from all unrighteousness (1 John 1:9). I pray that no consequences of my sins be passed on to my child.

֍

Therefore, if anyone is in Christ, he is a new creation; old things have passed away; behold, all things have become new.

2 CORINTHIANS 5:17

Destroying an Inheritance
of Family Bondage

Lord, I pray that no work of the enemy in my family's past will be able to encroach upon the life of my child, (name of child), today. I pray specifically about (name something you see in yourself or your family that you don't want passed on to your child). Whatever is not Your will for our lives, I reject as sin.

Thank You, Jesus, that You came to set us free from the past. We refuse to live bound by it. I pray that my son (daughter) will not inherit any bondage from his (her) earthly family, but will inherit the kingdom prepared for him [her] from the foundation of the world (Matthew 25:34).

Thank You, Jesus, that in You the old has passed away and all things are new.

Stand fast therefore in the liberty by which Christ has made us free, and do not be entangled again with a yoke of bondage.

GALATIANS 5:1

Avoiding Alcohol, Drugs, and Other Addictions

*L*ord, I pray that You would keep (name of child) free from any addiction—especially to alcohol or drugs. Make her (him) strong in You, draw her (him) close and enable her (him) to put You in control of her (his) life. Speak to her (his) heart, show her (him) the path she (he) should walk, and help her (him) see that protecting her (his) body from things that destroy it is a part of her (his) service to You.

Lord, You have said that If you live according to the flesh you will die; but if by the Spirit you put to death the deeds of the body, you will live (Romans 8:13). Teach her (him) to live by the Spirit and not the flesh.

I have set before you life and death, blessing and cursing; therefore choose life, that both you and your descendants may live.

DEUTERONOMY 30:19

Avoiding Alcohol, Drugs, and Other Addictions

*L*ord, I pray that You would thwart any plan Satan has to destroy her (his) life through alcohol and drugs. Take away anything in her (his) personality that would be drawn to those substances. Your Word says, There is a way that seems right to a man, but its end is the way of death (Proverbs 16:25). Give her (him) discernment and strength to be able to say no to things that bring death and yes to the things of God that bring life.

May she (he) clearly see the truth whenever tempted and be delivered from the evil one whenever trapped. Enable her (him) to choose life in whatever she (he) does, and may her (his) only addiction be to the things of God. In Jesus' name I pray that everything she (he) does with her (his) body be done to Your glory.

The righteousness of the upright will deliver them, but the unfaithful will be caught by their lust.

PROVERBS 11:6

Rejecting Sexual Immorality

*L*ord, I pray that You will keep (name of child) sexually pure all of his (her) life. Give him (her) a heart that wants to do what's right in this area, and let purity take root in his (her) personality and guide his (her) actions.

Open his (her) eyes to the truth of Your Word, and help him (her) to see that sex outside of marriage will never be the committed, lasting, unconditional love that he (she) needs. Let his (her) personality not be scarred nor his (her) emotions damaged by the fragmentation of the soul that happens as a result of sexual immorality.

Put a Holy Spirit alarm in him (her) that goes off like a loud, flashing siren whenever he (she) steps over the line of what is right in Your sight.

This is the will of God, your sanctification: that you should abstain from sexual immorality.

1 THESSALONIANS 4:3

Rejecting Sexual Immorality

*L*ord, I pray that You would speak loudly to (name of child) whenever there is temptation to do something he (she) shouldn't, and make him (her) strong enough in You to stand for what's right. Help him (her) to resist temptation and say no to sexual immorality.

I pray that he (she) will have no premarital sex and will resist having sex with anyone other than his (her) marriage partner.

I pray that homosexuality will never take root in him (her) or even have an opportunity to express itself toward him (her). Protect him (her) from any sexual molestation. May Your grace enable him (her) to be committed to staying pure all the days of his (her) life.

Blessed is the man who endures temptation; for when he has been approved, he will receive the crown of life which the Lord has promised to those who love Him.

JAMES 1:12

Finding the
Perfect Mate

*L*ord, I pray that unless Your plan is for (name of child) to remain single, You will send the perfect marriage partner for her (him). Send the right husband (wife) at the perfect time, and give her (him) a clear leading from You as to who it is.

I pray that my daughter (son) will be submissive enough to hear Your voice when it comes time to make a marriage decision, and that she (he) will make that decision based on what You are saying and not just fleshly desire.

I pray that she (he) will trust You with all her (his) heart and lean not on her (his) own understanding; that she (he) will acknowledge You in all her (his) ways so that You will direct her (his) path (Proverbs 3:5-6). May she (he) have one wonderful mate for life.

Whoever divorces his wife and marries another commits adultery against her.

MARK 10:11

Finding the
Perfect Mate

⁓≈⁓

*L*ord, I pray that You would prepare the person who will make the perfect husband (wife) for (name of child). Help her (him) to know the difference between simply falling in love and knowing for certain this is the person with whom God wants her (him) to spend the rest of her (his) life. If she (he) becomes attracted to someone she (he) shouldn't marry, I pray that You, Lord, would cut off the relationship.

I pray that she (he) will marry a godly and devoted servant of Yours, who loves You and lives Your way, and will be a blessing to all other family members. May they be mutually loyal, compassionate, considerate, sensitive, respectful, affectionate, forgiving, supportive, caring, and loving toward one another all the days of their lives.

⁓≈⁓

There are many plans in a man's heart, nevertheless the Lord's counsel—that will stand.

PROVERBS 19:21

Living Free
of Unforgiveness

❧

*L*ord, I pray that You would enable (name of child) to live in ongoing forgiveness. Teach him (her) the depth of your forgiveness toward him (her) so that he (she) can be freely forgiving toward others. Help him (her) to make the decision to forgive based on what You've asked us to do and not on what feels good at the moment.

May he (she) understand that forgiveness doesn't justify the other person's actions; instead, it makes him (her) free. Help him (her) to understand that only You know the whole story about any of us, and that's why he (she) doesn't have the right to judge.

Teach him (her) to release the past to You so that he (she) can move into all that You have for him (her).

❧

Let all bitterness, wrath, anger, clamor, and evil speaking be put away from you, with all malice. And be kind to one another, tenderhearted, forgiving one another, even as God in Christ forgave you.

EPHESIANS 4:31-32

Living Free
of Unforgiveness

❦

*L*ord, I pray that (name of child) will never harbor resentment, bitterness, anger, or unforgiveness toward anyone.

I also pray that he (she) will forgive himself (herself) for times of failure, and may he (she) never blame You, Lord, for things that happen on this earth and in his (her) life. According to Your Word I pray that he (she) will love his (her) enemies, bless those who curse him (her), do good to those who hate him (her), and pray for those who spitefully use and persecute him (her), so that he (she) may enjoy all Your blessings (Matthew 5:44-45).

In Jesus' name, I pray that he (she) will live in the fullness of Your forgiveness for him (her) and the freedom of forgiveness toward others.

❦

Whenever you stand praying, if you have anything against anyone, forgive him, that your Father in heaven may also forgive you your trespasses.

MARK 11:25

Walking in Repentance

❧❧❧

*L*ord, I pray that You would give (name of child) a heart that is quick to confess her (his) mistakes. May she (he) be truly repentant of them so that she (he) can be forgiven and cleansed. Help her (him) to understand that Your laws are for her (his) benefit and that the confession and repentance You require must become a way of life.

Give her (him) the desire to live in truth before You, and may she (he) say as David did, Wash me thoroughly from my iniquity, and cleanse me from my sin. Create in me a clean heart, O God, and renew a steadfast spirit within me. Do not cast me away from Your presence, and do not take Your Holy Spirit from me. Restore to me the joy of Your salvation (Psalm 51:2,10-12).

❧❧❧

He who covers his sins will not prosper, but whoever confesses and forsakes them will have mercy.

PROVERBS 28:13

Walking
in Repentance

*L*ord, I pray that You would bring to light any hidden sins in (name of child) so they can be confessed, repented of, and forgiven.

I pray that my daughter (son) will never be able to contain sin within her (him), but rather let there be a longing to confess fully and say, See if there is any wicked way in me, and lead me in the way everlasting (Psalm 139:24).

May she (he) not live in guilt and condemnation, but rather dwell with a clear conscience in the full understanding of her (his) forgiveness in Christ. I pray that she (he) will always look to You and wear a radiant countenance.

> *Beloved, if our heart does not condemn us, we have confidence toward God. And whatever we ask we receive from Him, because we keep His commandments and do those things that are pleasing in His sight.*

1 JOHN 3:21-22

Breaking Down
Ungodly Strongholds

$\mathscr{L}$ord, I thank You that You have promised in Your Word to deliver us when we cry out to You. I come to You on behalf of (name of child) and ask that You would deliver him (her) from any ungodliness that may be threatening to become a stronghold in his (her) life.

Even though I don't know what he (she) needs to be set free from, You do. I pray in the name of Jesus that You will work deliverance in his (her) life wherever it is needed. I know that although we walk in the flesh, we do not war according to the flesh. For the weapons of our warfare are not carnal but mighty in God for pulling down strongholds, casting down arguments and every high thing that exalts itself against the knowledge of God (2 Corinthians 10:3-5). I depend on You, Lord, to give me wisdom and revelation. Show me anything I need to see regarding him (her).

There is nothing covered that will not be revealed,
and hidden that will not be known.

MATTHEW 10:26

Breaking Down
Ungodly Strongholds

~~~

*L*ord, I put (name of child) in Your hands this day. Guide, protect, and convict him (her) when sin is trying to take root. Strengthen him (her) in battle when Satan attempts to gain a foothold in his (her) heart. Make him (her) sensitive to enemy encroachment, and may he (she) run to You to be his (her) stronghold and refuge in times of trouble.

According to Your Word I say that You, Lord, will deliver him (her) from every evil work and preserve him (her) for Your heavenly kingdom (2 Timothy 4:18).

Let all that is hidden come to light. If there is any action I need to take, I depend on You to show me. Thank You that You help me parent this child.

~~~

I will give you the keys of the kingdom of heaven, and whatever you bind on earth will be bound in heaven, and whatever you loose on earth will be loosed in heaven.

MATTHEW 16:19

Seeking Godly Wisdom
and Discernment

⊰≈⊱

$\mathscr{L}$ord, I pray that You would give the gifts of wisdom, discernment, and revelation to (name of child). Help her (him) to trust You with all her (his) heart, not depending on her (his) own understanding, but acknowledging You in all her (his) ways so that she (he) may hear Your clear direction as to which path to take (Proverbs 3:5-6).

Help her (him) to discern good from evil and be sensitive to the voice of the Holy Spirit saying, This is the way, walk in it (Isaiah 30:21).

I know that much of her (his) happiness in life depends on gaining wisdom and discernment, which Your Word says brings long life, wealth, recognition, protection, enjoyment, contentment, and happiness. May all these things come to her (him) because of Your gift of wisdom.

⊰≈⊱

A wise son makes a glad father, but a foolish son is the grief of his mother.

PROVERBS 10:1

Seeking Godly Wisdom and Discernment

Lord, Your Word says, The fear of the LORD is the beginning of wisdom, and the knowledge of the Holy One is understanding (Proverbs 9:10). May a healthy fear and knowledge of You be the foundation upon which wisdom and discernment are established in (name of child).

May she (he) turn to You for all decisions so that she (he) doesn't make poor choices. Help her (him) to see that all the treasures of wisdom and knowledge are hidden in You and that You give of them freely when we ask for them.

As she (he) seeks wisdom and discernment from You, Lord, pour it liberally upon her (him) so that all her (his) paths will be peace and life.

Happy is the man who finds wisdom, and the man who gains understanding; for her proceeds are better than the profits of silver, and her gain than fine gold.

PROVERBS 3:13-14

Growing
in Faith

*L*ord, You have said in Your Word that You have dealt to each one a measure of faith (Romans 12:3). I pray that You would take the faith You have planted in (name of child) and multiply it. May the truth of Your Word be firmly established in his (her) heart so that faith will grow daily and navigate his (her) life. Help him (her) to trust You at all times as he (she) looks to You for truth, guidance, and transformation into Your likeness. May his (her) faith be the substance of things hoped for, the evidence of things not seen (Hebrews 11:1).

I pray he (she) will have faith strong enough to lift him (her) above his (her) circumstances and limitations and instill in him (her) the confidence of knowing that everything will work together for good.

Whatever things you ask when you pray, believe that you receive them, and you will have them.

MARK 11:24

Growing in Faith

*L*ord, I pray that (name of child) will be so strong in faith that his (her) relationship with You supersedes all else in his (her) life—even my influence as a parent. In other words, may he (she) have a relationship with You, Lord, that is truly his (her) own—not an extension of mine or anyone else's.

I want the comfort of knowing that when I'm no longer on this earth, his (her) faith will be strong enough to keep him (her) steadfast, immovable, always abounding in the work of the Lord (1 Corinthians 15:58).

I pray that he (she) will take the shield of faith in order to quench all the fiery darts of the wicked one (Ephesians 6:16).

If you have faith as a mustard seed, you will say to this mountain, Move from here to there, and it will move; and nothing will be impossible for you.

MATTHEW 17:20

Other Books
by Stormie Omartian

∾∾∾

THE POWER OF A PRAYING® HUSBAND
The Power of a Praying® Husband
The Power of a Praying® Husband Book of Prayers
The Power of a Praying® Husband Prayer & Study Guide
The Power of a Praying® Husband Deluxe Edition

THE POWER OF A PRAYING® PARENT
The Power of a Praying® Parent
The Power of a Praying® Parent Book of Prayers
The Power of a Praying® Parent Prayer and Study Guide
The Power of a Praying® Parent Deluxe Edition

THE POWER OF A PRAYING® WIFE
The Power of a Praying® Wife
The Power of a Praying® Wife Audio Book
The Power of a Praying® Wife Book of Prayers
The Power of a Praying® Wife Prayer and Study Guide
The Power of a Praying® Wife Deluxe Edition

THE POWER OF A PRAYING® WOMAN
The Power of a Praying® Woman
The Power of a Praying® Woman Bible
The Power of a Praying® Woman Book of Prayers
The Power of a Praying® Woman Prayer and Study Guide
The Power of a Praying® Woman Deluxe Edition

JUST ENOUGH LIGHT FOR THE STEP I'M ON
Just Enough Light for the Step I'm On
Just Enough Light for the Step I'm On—
A Devotional Prayer Journey
Just Enough Light for the Step I'm On
Book of Prayer

THE PRAYER THAT CHANGES EVERYTHING®

The Prayer That Changes Everything®
The Prayer That Changes Everything®
Book of Prayers
The Prayer That Changes Everything®
Prayer Cards
The Prayer That Changes Everything® Audio Book

THE POWER OF PRAYER TO CHANGE YOUR MARRIAGE

The Power of Prayer to Change Your Marriage
The Power of Prayer to Change Your Marriage
Audio Book
The Power of Prayer to Change Your Marriage
Book of Prayers
The Power of Prayer to Change Your Marriage
Prayer and Study Guide

CHILDREN'S BOOKS

For This Child I Prayed
What Happens When I Talk to God?
Prayers and Promises for Little Boys
Prayers and Promises for Little Girls

OTHER ITEMS

A Book of Prayer
Greater Health God's Way
Prayers for Emotional Wholeness
Praying Through the Bible
The Power of a Praying® Kid
The Power of a Praying® Nation
The Power of a Praying® Teen
The Power of Praying®
The Power of Praying® Gift Collection
The Power of Praying® Together
Stormie

❧❧❧

www.stormieomartian